GOLDEN TIPS

A DESCRIPTION OF
CEYLON
AND ITS GREAT TEA INDUSTRY

HENRY W. CAVE

ILLUSTRATED FROM PHOTOGRAPHS BY THE AUTHOR

ISBN : 978-93-5324-569-6 (HB)

First Published, London, 1900

Published, 2020

Published by

Facsimile Publisher
12 Pragati Market
Ashok Vihar, Ph-2
Delhi-110052
E-mail: books@facsimilepublisher.com

Printed at: G. Print Process, Delhi.

Golden Tips
A Description of Ceylon
And its Great Tea Industry

Author: Henry W. Cave

GOLDEN TIPS.

A DESCRIPTION OF

Ceylon and its great Tea Industry.

BY

HENRY W. CAVE,

M.A., F.R.G.S.,

MEMBER OF THE ROYAL ASIATIC SOCIETY,

Author of "The Ruined Cities of Ceylon," "Colombo and the Kelani Valley," "Kandy and Peradeniya," "Nuwara Eliya and Adam's Peak."

ILLUSTRATED FROM PHOTOGRAPHS BY THE AUTHOR.

LONDON:

SAMPSON LOW, MARSTON AND COMPANY, LIMITED,

ST. DUNSTAN'S HOUSE,

FETTER LANE, FLEET STREET, E.C.

1900.

PREFACE.

"I KNOW it is the opinion of the present Governor,* and of leading colonists and officials, that Ceylon only needs to be better and more widely known to be still more appreciated."

To these words of Mr. John Ferguson, spoken before a great assembly at the Royal Colonial Institute, I reply with this humble contribution, designed to assist in creating the greater knowledge and appreciation regarded as needful by such eminent authorities.

A word of reference to my previous works on Ceylon is necessary to explain the connection of this book with them. The public has eagerly possessed itself of the first editions of four costly volumes, and from this it may be inferred that the subjects and method of dealing with them are attractive. It is, moreover, reasonable to suppose that had the price been within the reach of everybody a larger circulation would have resulted. I have been led by these considerations to adhere to the same plan of

* The Right Honourable Sir J. West Ridgeway, G.C.M.G., K.C.B., K.C.S.I.

illustrating all my descriptions with photographs, so placed that they can at once be seen together with the text to which they refer. Further than this, I have introduced a few of the illustrations and some of the text from my previous books in places where I have been unable to improve on either, and yet felt it necessary to go over the same ground.

I have avoided statistics as far as possible; but where I have found it necessary to introduce them I have been guided by the valuable "Handbook and Directory of Ceylon" by Mr. John Ferguson.

For assistance in technical matters connected with the culture of the tea plant and the processes of manufacture I am indebted to many friends, and especially Mr. J. Stewart, on whose estate, in the Agras, the various studies of field and factory work were made.

"We" throughout this book generally means the reader and the author, and very seldom the author only.

HENRY W. CAVE.

NUWARA ELIYA,
SEPTEMBER, 1900.

CONTENTS.

*

ILLUSTRATIONS.

GOLDEN TIPS.

CHAPTER I.

INTRODUCTORY.

THE great tea industry of Ceylon, although an enterprise of recent growth, has become an important item of the world's commerce. The extraordinary rapidity with which this latest product of the resplendent Lanka has gained universal favour is, of course, due to its superiority over the pekoes and souchongs of other countries. General interest in the island has been quickened to a remarkable extent by its phenomenal success, and those who drink the "cup that cheers" now wish to learn more of the country that produces such an excellent and dainty beverage. It is the desire of the author to supply the wished-for information, and fortunately for his purpose this branch of agriculture lends itself admirably to pictorial and literary treatment.

It would be difficult to produce an attractive book upon wheat-growing in the plains of Dakota, or any other extensive agricultural industry depending upon the labour of the white man. Such subjects would be prosaic and wanting in the picturesque. But tea culture in Ceylon is associated with life in a tropical country of unrivalled beauty and interest, "where every prospect pleases" and where the operations of agriculture are carried on under conditions and amidst surroundings that cannot fail to appear novel and interesting to those for whom these pages are written.

The planter will find little here that is unfamiliar to him; he knows the scenes and operations described; to him the motley throng of "muster" in the grey dawn of twilight, or the pretty picture of the dusky maidens sorting their freshly plucked leaf at dewy eve, are things of his daily round, familiar and disregarded: but who amongst his friends in the old country would not regard any one of these scenes with great interest and curiosity?

During the years 1886 to 1897 I received, in England, a large number of letters requesting information about tea planting in Ceylon. Many of my correspondents were merely seeking opportunities for investment; others sought information as to the prospects which the colony offered their sons who wished to learn tea-planting; while nearly all wished for any information I could give about the healthiness or unhealthiness of the climate and life in the tea districts. These requests, if they have not directly led me to write this book, will greatly influence the plan and the matter of it. While describing the country and its chief industry I shall especially dwell upon matters about which I have repeatedly been questioned.

We shall not concern ourselves with the history of tea drinking or detail here all those well-known stories about the discovery of tea in China nearly five thousand years ago; its certain use in that country twelve centuries ago; its introduction into Europe by the Dutch in the early part of the seventeenth century; its supposed pernicious use in England, a few years later, as more degrading than excess of wine and tobacco after dinner; or Dr. Johnson's eulogies on the cup that cheered him by day and solaced him in midnight toil. We know that tea has been the favourite beverage of the intellectual during the age of letters and that its praises have been sung by the most cultured of the human race; and we might fill pages with description of its uses and appreciation for centuries before the soil of Ceylon was ever called upon to produce a single tea plant. Our province, however, is to deal with the Ceylon article, and our references to the commodity as produced by other countries need only be made by way of comparison, to prove, if need be, the superiority of the Ceylon product in both cultivation and manufacture. Even this would seem a needless task in face of the fact that on its merits the Ceylon tea industry has developed with a rapidity unequalled even by that of India, which started many years earlier and which began to oust from the best markets the enormous supplies of China.

Our history will, therefore, be confined to the Ceylon product of the last twenty years. It is true that the plant was introduced into Ceylon before this time. A field was planted in Rambodde pass as early as 1842, but no real attempt to make it a commercial success appears to have been made till the eighties, when necessity gave the impetus owing to the coffee failures, which by that time were regarded as insurmountable. Yet both the Government and the Planters' Association had been mindful of the fact that tea had been planted and would grow in Ceylon: the former sent a commissioner to Assam to study its cultivation and report upon it; and the latter, acting upon the report, entered upon further experiments in the sixties. The author remembers passing through some experimental tea gardens in the Rambodde district in 1877, but little progress had by that time been made and practically nothing had been done in local manufacture. The cultivation of cinchona at this time reached a fever heat and was so rapidly successful as to cause its own failure as a permanent commercial success by over-production. Then followed the first excitement about Ceylon tea, and the subsequent rapid development of the great industry.

These few remarks will suffice by way of introduction, and I now invite the reader to accept my services as cicerone. In the following pages he may accompany me to all those parts of Ceylon which have attracted the colonist; see what he has done, what he is doing, and how he does it, and besides this he may see and hear something about those general features of the country and the life of its inhabitants which are so attractive to European visitors. And first of all we must deal with Colombo, that port which within a few years has become one of the most important to British commerce generally and is particularly associated with the experiences, social and commercial, of every European who has lived in Ceylon.

"WE GLANCE FOR A MOMENT AT THE NOBLE BREAKWATER" (*page* 6).

CHAPTER II.

COLOMBO.

TO the early riser who is fortunate enough to arrive off the coast of Colombo at break of day the first scene that unfolds itself is one of unique beauty and for our purpose instructive. Let me describe my own oft-repeated experience. We have spent the last night on board. The good ship has brought us seven thousand miles in safety, and with grateful hearts we have toasted the captain at our last dinner, praising his seamanship, his geniality, his tact and his thoughtful care for us all throughout a month's pleasant voyage. The passengers for the more distant ports have drunk to us their departing friends, and we have spent the last merry hours with them, perchance never to meet again. And as midnight is signalled by four bells we lay our weary heads to rest for a few more hours on the spacious deck, where the tropical breezes fan us gently to sleep, until the first glimmer of dawn, when "swabbing the decks" begins. We would fain sleep on; but the relentless regulation which determines the slumbers of the passengers who choose the deck for their couch brings the hose swishing around us, and, rubbing our eyes, we arise and wander for'ard to the fo'c'sle.

From this point of vantage we look ahead and behold first the mountain zone "where the tea comes from" rising in one mighty upheaval from the plains of Ceylon, capped in the centre by the venerated peak named after our first parent. The mists are as yet lying in the valleys, and the cool blue tones above them give us the true contour of those fertile mountains upon which millions of tea bushes are flourishing. At different elevations there are four extensive ledges which appear to rise abruptly from the base, and from these a number of lofty mountains raise their rugged brows to the height of 5,000 to 8,000 feet. Here we get the best idea of the formation of those highlands which we shall presently explore, and whose deep ravines and grassy plains, dense forests and open valleys, gentle streams and roaring cataracts, besides their tens of thousands of acres of tea, we shall see in the full detail of close inspection.

As we approach nearer and nearer we see the mists arise, attracted upwards by the rays of the rising sun, and a scene of verdant loveliness is disclosed which stands in welcome contrast to the parched and barren shores we have left behind at Suez and Aden. The mountains are now lost to view and the particulars of the beautiful palm-fringed shore gradually increase as we steam towards the harbour, until at length the eye is filled by the intense luxuriance of the life and light that combine to greet us.

As we enter the harbour we glance for a moment at the noble breakwater which the genius of Sir John Coode fixed so firmly in the ocean bed that year after year it withstands the fury of monsoons

"THIS MOTLEY FLEET IS THE FIRST SCENE OF NOVELTY" (*page 12*).

which hurl their terrific mountains of sea against its ever resisting concrete mass. The construction of this breakwater was begun in the year of the Prince of Wales' visit to Ceylon, 1875, and his Royal Highness laid the foundation stone. It is 4,000 feet long and shelters a water area of 500 acres. Although it forms but a part of the complete scheme of a harbour and graving dock, it has been of immense value to the colony, not only in protecting from the fury of the elements the ships that bring our foreign supplies and carry our produce away; but in attracting the shipping of the Eastern world, as well as the colonies, by the convenience it offers as a coaling station and junction for exchange of passengers. The northern arm and graving dock, both of which are now in course of construction, will perfect the accommodation, and give to Colombo one of the largest and safest artificial harbours in the world. The shipping trade that is now carried on within this port would have been impossible in the seventies, when every vessel was compelled to anchor in the open roadstead, and to embark and discharge in sea that was often rough and sometimes dangerous.

But we have now arrived within the harbour, and our attention is arrested by many quaint scenes. A myriad canoes are making for our vessel from the shore. Their singular form excites our immediate interest. Each is constructed from the trunk of a tree, which is first hollowed out and then levelled at the top. Safe balance is secured by an outrigger attachment, which consists of two poles of wood extending at right angles to a distance of about ten feet from the body of the boat, and connected at the ends by a float. Our illustration on page 9 will give a better idea of them than verbal description. Boats of this construction are used almost universally by the Singhalese for fishing and for passenger traffic. They withstand the roughest sea, and literally fly before the breeze. As each steamer drops anchor within the magnificent breakwater of Colombo these curiously constructed craft crowd around, many of them bringing traders laden with precious stones, which will be offered at double or treble their value to unwary passengers; others plying for the hire of their boats to take passengers ashore; some with dusky Tamils, who sing unceasingly to the plash of their oars; many with comely Singhalese of lighter complexion, their long hair twisted into a thick knot surmounted by a tortoiseshell comb, giving them a curiously feminine appearance; some with Indo-Arab traders in their curious costumes of many colours, and their shaven heads crowned with tall plaited brimless hats of many-coloured silks. This motley fleet is the first scene of novelty that claims attention upon arrival in the harbour of Colombo.

Our next proceeding is to go ashore, where we no sooner set our foot than we are impressed with the luxurious aspect of the place. The streets are broad; the roads are good; the merchants' offices and stores are capacious and in many instances possess considerable architectural merit, while the hotels are infinitely superior to any others in the East, a matter of no small interest and importance to the traveller and resident alike. The Grand Oriental Hotel faces the harbour and is the first building to attract attention. Our illustration will give some idea of its

THE GRAND ORIENTAL HOTEL

proportions. A wise traveller never sets out unequipped with information about the caravanserais where he will perforce be compelled to halt, and upon whose qualities, good, bad or indifferent, much of his enjoyment will be found to depend. Neither must we disregard places of such importance from any fear of seeming to advertise them. The G. O. H., as this fine hotel is familiarly called, commands the best view of the harbour and shipping. It will repay us to ascend to the roof, where we shall get some idea of shipping operations in the gorgeous East.

Hundreds of pairs of Indian humped-bulls are drawing down thousands of chests of Ceylon tea; dusky Tamil and Singhalese coolies are receiving it into boats and conveying it to the steamers. Every stroke of work ashore or oar afloat is accompanied by an inordinate amount of jabber. The tongue of the harbour coolie seems to move automatically, but we are told that the soft tones which he ejaculates could not be translated into English: we have no words or phrases sufficiently shocking for the purpose. However as we do not understand him we are not offended; while his methods and proceedings amuse us.

Ceylon being ethnographically part of India many customs are alike in both, and amongst them is the one of separate business localities for natives and Europeans. We therefore find in Colombo a large area occupied almost exclusively by Government and merchants' offices; the Queen's House, the residence of the Governor of the Colony; and the military quarters. The last named consist of five blocks of handsome barracks, unequalled in any other part of the East in point of healthy situation, design and construction. This part of Colombo, which consists of a block of about half a dozen fine streets, is known as the Fort, although there is nothing visible now to suggest that appellation. It was such, however, in earlier times, and we may pause for a moment to inquire briefly into its history.

About the year 1505 the Portuguese landed at Colombo and built stores and factories for trading purposes. Kotte, six miles distant, was then the seat of native government, and it is doubtful whether Colombo itself was more than a coast village of modest thatched huts. The Portuguese, however, must have rapidly developed it in importance and extent. They soon constructed works to protect their factories, and as the latter extended they increased and strengthened their fort until its walls mounted two hundred guns and was impregnable to the native army of 50,000 men and 2,000 elephants which besieged it for two years. But it was not until the Dutch had ousted the Portuguese from Ceylon that the splendid fort which the British have gradually demolished was constructed. Within the last thirty years the massive walls have disappeared; the moat has been filled in, and upon the site of the great eighteenth century fortress has risen the "Fort" of to-day, a compact commercial city.

The settlements of the Portuguese and Dutch were limited to a string of forts and factories around the coast with small seaboard territories. Upon our visits to Jaffna, Galle, Trincomali and other coast towns we shall see some of these and gain from them a very good impression of the excellence of Dutch masonry.

The finest building in the Fort is the Post Office, and the finest street is that in which it is situated, namely, Queen Street. Here are to be found the residence of the Governor of the colony, some of the principal banks, the lighthouse, and many merchants' offices. It will be noticed in looking at our photographs that many of the buildings are hidden from view by Suriya trees. The roads, which are made of dark red cabook, are in almost every street thus shaded. A combination of colour is

THE GENERAL POST OFFICE.

thus formed which is most effective in softening the tropical glare, and renders it possible to look upon the surrounding objects with comfort, even under the powerful rays of the mid-day sun. The Suriya tree (*Thespesia Populnea*) flowers profusely with delicate primrose-coloured blossoms, large and showy, changing to purple as they fade. In form they somewhat resemble the single scarlet hibiscus. In some of the streets the charm of variety has been attained by the introduction of other beautiful shade-trees amongst the Suriyas.

Our view of Queen Street (central) shows the Mercantile Bank beneath the trees on the right, and beyond it a handsome block of buildings, the commercial house of the Caves, founded by the author in the seventies. We have referred to, and illustrated, the Post Office, which is in the same street. Opposite this is the Queen's House, too much embowered in foliage for a photograph; and adjoining

QUEEN STREET, COLOMBO.

is a fine terraced garden, the Jubilee gift of the Hon. Sir Arthur Hamilton Gordon (now Lord Stanmore). This is the brightest spot in the Fort; for there all manner of feathery palms, gorgeous crotons, and rosy oleanders combine to lend colour and fragrance to a charming corner of the European quarter. There are other fine buildings in this broad and handsome street, notably the Hong-kong and Shanghai Bank and the offices of the Government.

A picturesque corner of the Fort is the western end of Prince's Street, where will be noticed in our illustration (page 23) the offices of the famous Lipton, Limited. Our photograph looks eastward and the distant road leads from the European merchants' quarter to that of the natives, called the Pettah, with which we shall deal later.

Quite worthy of notice in our view of York Street is a building, recently erected, called the Victoria

YORK STREET, COLOMBO

Arcade. This fine block covers a portion of the old Dutch moat. At one end of it are the offices of the Peninsular and Oriental Navigation Company and at the other end the National Bank of India, while between them runs an arcade fitted up with shops, occupied by dealers in gems and curiosities, upper stories of offices and residential flats. In the distant part of our view of this street is another excellent hotel, the Bristol, and several stores. Half way up this street at right angles is Baillie Street, narrower than those we have described, but not less important in its commercial features; for here are to be found the Bank of Madras and many of the large mercantile offices: it is one of the busiest and most crowded thoroughfares in all the Fort. A little further on, and parallel with it, runs Chatham Street where the lighthouse again comes into view. Along this street pass, in one continuous

CHATHAM STREET, COLOMBO.

stream from morning till night, curious palm-thatched carts laden with produce for shipment.

Amongst recent valuable additions to the mercantile buildings in the Fort not the least important is the fine block erected for the accommodation of the Chamber of Commerce. This society was established in Colombo in the year 1837 to protect the interests of the colony's trade. All the important mercantile firms are represented in its deliberations. It gives authority to rates of agency and commission; it fixes a standard tonnage scale for all classes of produce; arranges rules and conditions of produce sales; nominates surveyors, arbitrators and umpires, thereby giving an official character to their reports and awards; and assists the Government by its discussions and resolutions upon commercial matters which are in need of legislation. Its influence in this last direction is important and considerable, and is rendered the more effective by the circumstance that its wishes are made known in the legislative assemblies by the Mercantile Member of the Council who is practically its own representative.

The merchants of Colombo may well be proud of the transformation of the old Dutch Fort. The greatest improvements are of the last few years' growth, and may be said to be mainly due to the success of the tea industry. We have, however, noticed many extensive buildings in course of erection, which is a satisfactory sign that, although the present features of the place are so excellent, "advance" is the key-note still sounding, and every year seems likely to witness still more important developments. But the Colombo merchant's sphere is not limited to the Fort. Each mercantile house has its mills in the suburbs, where the produce is received and prepared for shipment. This subject, as far as tea is concerned, will be touched upon later. We may, however, here take cognisance of the extensive range of minor products that form an important part of the Colombo merchants' trade. We shall notice them but briefly as a slight diversion from our main subject.

The produce of the palms is next in importance

to tea, and especially that of the cocoanut. The increased use of this nut in confectionery during the last few years has greatly stimulated the export trade, and there are now mills in Colombo for desiccating as well as those for extracting oil and fibre. The uses of the cocoanut are so many that we cannot enumerate them, and it must suffice to note the extent of cultivation, the local consumption, and the export trade. It is estimated that considerably more than half a million acres are cultivated with this palm, and that the annual value of the produce is near £2,000,000 sterling. About a third of the nuts go through the various processes that produce oil, confectionery, copra and fibre for export; and the remainder are used locally for food and various manufactures. Another palm which yields valuable produce is the Palmyra, but it does not contribute much to the export trade. It grows principally in the drier regions of the north, and its edible products supply a very large proportion of the food of the inhabitants. The areca palm is next in importance, and in addition to a very large local consumption, provides an annual export of the value of about £100,000. Cacao, although the land suitable for its cultivation in Ceylon is of limited area, has reached an export of 40,000 cwt.; Cardamons amount to upwards of 500,000 lbs. annually; Coffee still claims a place worthy of account with its 13,000 or so hundred-weight a year; while Cinchona is exported to the full extent which the market demands—about a million lbs.

The oldest export of which Ceylon has any record is Cinnamon. It is indigenous, and may be found in a wild state in the oldest forests. In the Portu-

PRINCE'S STREET, COLOMBO

guese and Dutch periods this cultivated shrub was the principal source of wealth to the colonists. It is now cultivated to the full extent of profitable demand, amounting to a customs value of about £100,000 annually.

There is one mineral worthy of mention as forming an important item of the island's exports and a rapidly increasing one—plumbago. Ceylon is the chief source of supply for this mineral, and it is a fortunate circumstance that with increased "finds," and the consequent rapid extension of the industry, increased uses for plumbago are being discovered so rapidly that the supply is not likely to exceed the demand, as in case of some of the agricultural products. The annual yield of the mines already in working amounts to about thirty thousand tons, while the value of the best quality has risen to £75 a ton.

The gem quarries of Ceylon, of which there are upwards of four hundred, scarcely call for our consideration, as it is impossible to gauge the extent or value of the export trade in precious stones.

The business of the colony, both legislative and commercial, is chiefly transacted in the Fort. In the early days of the British rule the annual imports amounted to about £250,000. They are now about five millions. During the same period the revenue has risen from £226,000 to about one and a half million. In the early days there were no banks, no good roads or bridges, very few schools, no hospitals, only four post offices, and no newspapers. There are now fourteen important exchange and deposit banks and banking agencies doing an annual sum of business amounting to about seventy millions of rupees, fifteen hundred miles of splendid metalled roads, countless good bridges, more than two thousand schools, upwards of a hundred hospitals and dispensaries, two hundred and fifty post offices, thirty-six newspapers and periodicals, and nearly five millions of acres of land under cultivation. The shipping entered and cleared in the course of the year amounts to nearly six millions of tons, as against seventy-five thousand in the early part of the century.

From this recital of figures some idea may be gathered of the importance of the Fort as a business quarter, and of the present flourishing condition of the colony of Ceylon.

We will now visit the Pettah or native traders' quarter.

A SINGHALESE HACKERY.

CHAPTER III.

THE PETTAH.

EUROPEAN residents in Ceylon, as a rule, dislike passing through purely native streets, but the traveller finds many attractions in them, and is usually more interested by a drive through the Pettah than any other part of Colombo. An accomplished authoress has well described it as "an ever fascinating kaleidoscope." The numerous races of people represented: Singhalese, Moors, Tamils, Parsees, Dutch, Portuguese, Malays, and Afghans; the variety of costume worn by each race in accordance with caste or social position, from the simple loin cloth of the coolie to the gorgeous attire of the wealthy and high-caste gentleman; the different complexions and forms of toilet, and the avocations being carried on in the open street, are all entertaining to the visitor who for the first time becomes a witness of the manners and customs of oriental life. At every turn the eye is met by a fresh picture, and a new subject for study is presented to the mind. This mixed and motley crowd live their life and carry on their labours almost entirely in public. Neither doors, windows, nor shutters interfere with a complete view of the interior of their houses and stalls. The handicraftsman works serenely in his open shed, sometimes even in the open street; women are occupied in their most domestic affairs unveiled from the glance of the curious passer by, and tiny children, clothed only in the rich tints of their own complexions, sport amongst the traffic. All this harmonises charmingly with the conditions of climate and the nature of the people. The heat renders clothing uncomfortable, and closed up dwellings unendurable.

AVOCATIONS CARRIED ON IN THE OPEN STREET.

We find one street in this quarter so crowded that it is almost impossible to drive through it at any time of the day. It is the street of the Chetties, immigrants from southern India who deal in rice and cotton goods. They are a frugal and orderly people, many of them wealthy, and nearly all of them great usurers. They are first-class accountants, and some hold positions of trust as clerks in the banks and in the offices of European merchants. The rice dealers are conspicuous by the scantiness of their attire; they wear only a thin white muslin cloth, curiously arranged about their legs, and their heads are clean shaven and bare. The accountants, on the other hand, wear a white comboy and jacket, with a large number of buttons of sterling gold.

The native boutique, or provision shop, which abounds in the Pettah and all native quarters, is fairly represented in our picture. The open character of the whole street is of this nature, the stalls varying only in the classes of goods offered for sale.

NATIVE PROVISION SHOP.

Here there are fruits, curry stuffs of dried fish, various spices, earthernware chatties, and firewood. In another shop may be seen all manner of vegetables; and in others again gay comboys, or loin cloths, articles of native manufacture in brass-ware and pottery, and various useful articles made from the cocoa-nut and other palms. The money-changer's stalls, too, are perhaps the most purely Eastern of any, and are a prominent feature in these native bazaars.

Each little store is presided over by its owner, who almost invariably sits with his legs folded beneath him upon the sloping planks whereon his goods are displayed for sale. His customers are almost as varied as his wares. The Singhalese man, of sienna complexion, wearing his long hair gathered up into a knot surmounted by a comb of tortoise-shell, appears in various garb according to caste, even the comb assuming different forms in accordance with social position. The Singhalese women, too, have a multitude of distinctions both in dress and ornaments. Some of the highland women wear a single coloured cloth, which they wind about themselves in a very artistic fashion, leaving one shoulder bare. The lowland Singhalese women have two garments: the comboy, reaching from the waist to the ankles, and a short bodice with low-cut neck. All indulge, more or less, in jewellery, consisting of necklaces and bangles on both arms and ankles, and rings on their fingers and toes. They wear their hair twisted into a lump at the back of the head and secured by pins of ornamental patterns. Many Tamil women wear but a single coloured cloth, which they gracefully entwine about their limbs, leaving the right side bare to the hip; but some wear, in addition, a tightly-fitting jacket as shown in our plate. The very poor decorate themselves with ornaments of shells, sharks' teeth, beads, and berries. The costumes of the native men are even more varied. The Moormen with shaven heads, crowned with curiously plaited brimless hats of coloured silks, and gorgeous comboys; the Parsees in white calico and still more curious headgear; the Tamils with religious symbols upon their foreheads,

A STREET IN THE PETTAH

A TAMIL WOMAN

in white, black, red, or yellow, becoming turbans upon their heads, and the smallest possible quantity of clothing about their bodies, a square yard of coloured calico sufficing in most instances; the Afghans, contrasting with the Tamils in their superabundance of gaudy attire — such are the races, and such the dresses, of the native inhabitants of Colombo. They form very picturesque groups in the Pettah, which is at all times literally crowded with them; so much so that, when one is driving this way, the nimble muttu, or native groom, has to run the whole distance by the horse's head, keeping up a continual shouting to warn them out of the way.

LITTLE LUXURIES FOR PASSERS-BY.

THE COLOMBO CLUB AND THE GALLE FACE HOTEL.

CHAPTER IV.

RESIDENTIAL COLOMBO.

THE more extensive and more beautiful division of Colombo is that devoted to residential purposes and the recreation of the wealthier inhabitants. This may be said to cover about twenty square miles. Although it is almost entirely at sea-level, there being no hills in the neighbourhood, it is remarkably healthy and, for a tropical climate, temperate. It has a network of carriage roads, unequalled as such, and unique also in the abundance of beautiful vegetation with which they are bordered. There is choice of locality to suit various tastes and the requirements of differing constitutions. Those whom the strong sea air does not suit can find a milder atmosphere in the cinnamon gardens. Those of sporting or athletic tastes can live in the neighbourhood of the race-course, cricket grounds, or golf links, while those whose tastes can find no satisfaction in the conveniences and luxuries which this most beautiful of tropical cities affords have still an asylum of grand proportions open to them, thanks to the foresight of Sir James Longden.

As we leave the Fort by the seaside in a southerly direction we drive across a fine open green known as Galle Face, with the sea on one side and lake on the other. A fine esplanade extends the whole length, which is nearly a mile. Our photograph gives a view of the southern end with the Colombo Club on the left and another magnificent hotel on the right. Galle Face Hotel demands special notice as being the latest addition to the excellent hostel-

ENTRANCE HALL OF THE GALLE FACE HOTEL.

ries of Ceylon, and perhaps in many respects unequalled in the East. It is fitted in luxurious oriental style and enjoys the advantage of a site as perfect as could be obtained for the great desideratum of sea breeze. We give a view of the entrance-hall, which will convey some idea of the cool and spacious interior.

The road which leads past the hotel on the left continues along the coast for about one hundred miles, and in no part is it much less beautiful than the portion illustrated in our picture on page 41 entitled "The Galle Road." It passes through a forest of palms with frequent avenues at right angles, down which we catch glimpses of the shore. For the first three or four miles well-kept bungalows with large gardens, or compounds, as they are called, are noticeable at frequent intervals. These bungalows, which are the private residences of merchants,

THE GALLE ROAD AT PANEDURE.

civil servants, and some of the wealthier natives, are built in a very substantial manner of cabook stone walls, crowned with a high-pitched roof of red tiles, and surrounded by very deep verandahs, supported by rows of large white pillars. The verandahs generally occupy as much space as the rest of the bungalow, and are as a rule well furnished with luxurious lounges. They are much more used than the interior rooms, because they possess the advantages of outdoor life and yet afford complete protection from the sun.

The landscape in this direction varies little, however far we go, yet it is never wearisome. Every visitor is delighted with it: the naturalist is enchanted by the abundance of interesting objects at every turn; while to the enthusiastic botanist this highway, densely bordered on either side with an inexhaustible variety of leaf and blossom, is a treasury unsurpassed in any other country. The brown thatched huts, groups of gaily-clad natives, animals, birds—all these add life to a scene that baffles description. Garlands of creepers festooned from tree to tree; huge banyans stretching in archways completely over the road, with the stems all overgrown by ferns, orchids, and other parasitic plants; here and there a blaze of the flame-coloured gloriosa. golden orchids, various kinds of orange and lemon trees covered with fragrant blossoms, climbing lilies, an undergrowth of exquisite ferns of infinite variety, all crowned by slender palms of ninety or a hundred feet in height—it is vain to attempt a full description of such a scene.

A tree will be noticed in our illustration with lateral branches thrown out in groups of three, some feet apart, and bearing a large crop of pods on otherwise bare branches. This is the cotton tree, called by the Singhalese Katu-Imbul. It may be seen on this road in three stages; first, it becomes loaded with crimson blossoms before any leaves appear; then, the leaves develop; and afterwards it bears pods as seen in the picture. When ripe, the cotton bursts from the pod, and where the trees are uncultivated it strews the road; but where culti-

THE GALLE ROAD.

vation is carried on, it is collected from the pods, and the fibre, being too short for spinning, is used for various purposes locally, and is also exported to some extent for stuffing mattresses.

Perhaps the most popular residential part of Colombo is that lying to the left of the road which we have just described, half a mile farther inland. This locality is known as the Cinnamon Gardens, and consists of a park, laid out as a Jubilee Memorial to Queen Victoria, a magnificent race-course, and many miles of splendidly made red roads through groves of cinnamon and every kind of palm. The traveller is always impressed by the excellent condition of the roads in this locality. Their colour, so restful to the eye, is in charming contrast to the irrepressible greenery bordering and surrounding them on every hand. Each residence nestles in a paradise of palms and flowering shrubs of infinite variety, crotons most gorgeous and creepers innumerable, the latter overgrowing roofs and pillars and climbing the neighbouring trees, which they bespangle with their lovely blossoms. An evening drive through this part of Colombo is a botanical feast of the most exhilarating nature. In the part now known as the Victoria Park one may wander under the shade of palms and figs, or rest beneath clumps of graceful bamboo, surrounded by blossoms and perfumes of the most enchanting kind. The huge purple bells of the Thunbergia creep over the archways, and gorgeous passion flowers, orchids, pitcher plants, bright-leaved caladiums, and multitudes of other tropical plants everywhere flourish and abound.

One of the most charming features of Colombo is its fresh-water lake stretching over many hundreds of acres between the Fort and the Cinnamon Gardens. Its ramifications are so many that one is constantly coming across pretty nooks and corners quite unexpectedly, each fresh view presenting a wealth of foliage beyond description. An excellent road follows the winding course of the bank, and when in April the flowering trees are in blossom a drive in this direction is enchanting. Palms in

THE PALM-FRINGED BANKS.

great variety intermingle with the gorgeous mass of scarlet flamboyant blossoms, the lovely lemon-yellow lettuce tree, the ever graceful bamboo, the crimson blooms of the dark hibiscus, contrasting with the rich green of the areca, date, and palmyra palms, the huge waving leaves of the plantain, trees and shrubs of every description of tropical foliage—all these form a border of unrivalled beauty to the rippling waters.

We cannot dwell longer in this fascinating place, Colombo, although it were tempting to discuss every feature, since all differ so amazingly from the characteristics of old England. But we must away to the tea country.

KNUCKLE BONES.

SAINT CLAIR FALLS, DIMBULA.

CHAPTER V.

THE TEA COUNTRY.

THE Tea Estates of Ceylon, of which there are upwards of a thousand, varying in size from one hundred to a thousand acres each, and comprising a total of 370,000 acres, are divided into about sixty districts. For the most part these properties are situated in the mountainous central province of the island and vary in elevation above sea level from one hundred to seven thousand feet; there are, however, some extensive districts in the lowlands, notably the Kelani Valley, which, although younger as a planting district, has developed with such rapidity that it already claims equal importance with the most extensive divisions in the hills. A glance at our map will give an idea of the proportion of Ceylon under tea cultivation. We shall not need to discuss the characteristics of each district separately, nor yet adopt the principle of *ex uno disce omnes*, but taking a middle course we will select representative views, and illustrate processes of cultivation and manufacture in such parts as will give us a full and correct impression of the whole.

It will be seen from our map that the railway takes us into the heart of the mountain country and that the Kandyan district is one of the first we shall enter in our tour of inspection. Thousands of people who call at the port of Colombo on their voyage to Australia, or to other countries, find time for a trip to Kandy, the mountain capital of Ceylon; thousands more would do so if they knew how

LOWLAND VILLAGE SCENE

beautiful and how pleasantly accessible it is. To the foot of the mountain pass we travel through a fascinating panorama of lowland scenery. Those to whom this is the first experience of travel in a tropical country cannot fail to feel enchanted by the alternating scenes of quaint husbandry, glimpses of villages embosomed in palms, magnificent groups of tropical trees, and particularly with the effect of the deep recesses, occurring at frequent intervals, where cultivation extends between masses of grand forest.

We proceed somewhat rapidly through the lowlands, occasionally obtaining a glimpse of a young Tea Estate recently opened amidst the palm groves and rice fields, until at about the fiftieth mile the railway begins to ascend into the Kandyan mountains. The beauty of the landscape now heightens to the sublime; our pace is reduced to about eight

THE KANDYAN COUNTRY.

miles an hour, owing to the steepness of the gradient, and we are thus enabled to enjoy the panorama that unfolds itself as we move upward in winding and intricate course. The curves of the line are frequently so sharp that it is possible to see both the engines in front and the passengers seated in the last carriage behind. At one moment, on the edge of a sheer crag, we are gazing downwards some thousand feet below; at another we are looking upwards at a mighty crag a thousand feet above;

from the zigzags by which we climb the mountain sides fresh views appear at every turn; far-reaching valleys edged by the soft blue ranges of distant mountains and filled with luxuriant masses of dense forest, relieved here and there by the vivid green terraces of the rice fields; cascades of lovely flowering creepers, hanging in festoons from tree to tree and from crag to crag; deep ravines and foaming waterfalls above and below, dashing their spray into mist as it falls into the verdurous abyss; fresh mountain peaks appearing in ever-changing aspect as we gently wind along the steep gradients; sensational crossings from rock to rock, so startling as to unnerve the timid as we pass over gorges cleft in the mountain side, and look upon the green depths below, so near the edge of the vertical precipice that a fall from the carriage would land us sheer sixteen hundred feet below; the queen of palms, the lofty Talipot, which forms a lovely feature of this district, is flourishing on either side; the scattered huts and gardens, and the quaint people about them, so primitive in their habits that they vary little from the fashions of two thousand years ago—these are some of the features of interest as we journey into the Kandyan district.

Look for one moment, if you please, at our picture opposite showing the terraces which form little rice fields on the hillsides. This view is obtained as the train winds around the precipitous Allagalla depicted on page 53. Upon leaving this rock we reach the hill which is seen in our picture of the rice fields and as we wind around it we look back upon Allagalla, always majestic, but most beautiful immediately after excessive rainfall, when it is literally

"THE VIVID GREEN TERRACES OF THE RICE FIELDS" (*page* 50).

besprinkled with cataracts. On October 23rd, 1889, I last saw it in this condition. Rain had fallen heavily during the previous few days and now on a lovely bright morning I counted seventeen fine waterfalls, all within view at one time as the train passed round the hill adjoining Allagalla; some of them burst forth many hundreds of feet above the railway, which passes like a belt round the rock,

ALLAGALLA.

and dashed into the valleys some thousand feet below, increasing in volume and gathering enormous impetus as they passed under the line in deep fissures.

The height of Allagalla is 3,394 feet. Tea grows upon its steep acclivities, and those who are occupied in its cultivation on these giddy heights are enviable witnesses of the most varied and beautiful atmospheric scenes that are to be found in Ceylon. Unsettled weather is extremely frequent and is productive of an endless variety of cloud and storm effects over the wonderful valley which undulates below until in the far distance it is backed by the rugged mountains opposed to Allagalla and reaching greater height. At one time a vast sea of mists is rolling in fleecy clouds over the lowland acres and the summits of the hills are standing out from it like wooded islands; at another every shape of the beautiful landscape is faultlessly defined and every colour is vivid beneath the tropical sun; then an hour or two will pass and rolling masses of dense black vapours will approach the mountain while the sunbeams play on the distant hills; now the sun becomes obscured, a fiery streak dashes through the black mass and immediately the whole mountain seems shaken by the terrific peal of thunder—thunder of a quality that would turn any unaccustomed heart pale. Then follows a downpour at the rate of a full inch an hour; the cascades turn to roaring cataracts, the dry paths to rushing torrents and the rivulets to raging floods. The rice fields suddenly become transformed into lakes and the appearance of the valley suggests considerable devastation by water; but it is not so: the torrent passes away almost as suddenly as it comes and the somewhat bruised and battered vegetation freshens and bursts into new life as the heavy pall of purple cloud disperses and the gleams of the golden sun return to cheer its efforts. That tea or anything else should grow on these rocky slopes is one of the marvels of this wonderful land about which we shall have more to say later.

We are now in the freshness of mountain air and have left behind us the steamy low-country where the moist heat, although it is the efficient cause of the beautiful features of the landscape, is nevertheless very trying to our energies. For thirteen miles we have been slowly crawling round the mountain sides, ever moving upwards, till at length through a narrow pass we emerge upon one of those ledges of the mountain system to which we have previously referred.

For centuries the Kandyans held this pass against all attempts of Europeans to take their capital. Neither the Portuguese who occupied the maritime provinces in the sixteenth century, nor the Dutch by whom they were ousted in the seventeenth century, were ever able to conquer them. It is true that the Portuguese reached Kandy and even partly destroyed it, but were never able to hold it. At length the British drove out the Dutch in 1796, and permanently occupied Kandy somewhat later. But to gain possession of Kandy was by no means an easy task even for the British. The pretty mountain stronghold was destined to give much trouble to its new assailants and to be the scene of much bloodshed, treachery, and horrible barbarity before it was finally conquered. All this, however, is a matter of history fully dealt with by the author in another volume.* We are here concerned only with its present day aspect.

From Kadugannawa, the top of the pass, we have a nine miles' run into Kandy; passing by the Botanic Gardens of Peradeniya and several fine Tea Estates on either side.

We shall prefer to discuss the details of tea-

---

* "Kandy and Peradeniya," by Henry W. Cave. Demy 4to, illustrated. Sampson Low, Marston & Co.

growing when we reach still higher districts; but we must make more than passing reference to Kandy, which was once the great centre and capital of the planting country, and is now only less important because railways and roads have brought other districts, which it once served, into direct communication with Colombo. It is a municipal town of about twenty thousand inhabitants, of whom only about one hundred are English, about two or three hundred Eurasians, and the rest natives. It is the home of the planters' association, a society which is to the planting community what the chamber of commerce is to the merchants of Colombo; but having to guard the interests of a larger and more widely-spread community it has an extensive organisation which includes a completely representative parent committee and a special committee of thirty who watch over its interests in other parts of the world.

The formation of the town may be described as a deep basin in the hills, the bottom being covered by native quarters and a picturesque lake, around which many miles of carriage drives, bridle roads and walks, at various elevations embrace the hill-sides, which are studded with pretty bungalows. A reference to our photographs will give a correct idea of the way in which the beautiful little town clusters around the lake in all the luxuriance of foliage peculiar both to mountain and plain, for here they meet and mingle.

Kandy is pretty, but the Kandyan district is incomparably beautiful. The latter attribute is certainly applicable to the views from the roads, which wind around the hills on all sides and look down upon the far-reaching valleys, where the Mahawelli-ganga roils

THE PICTURESQUE LAKE OF KANDY.

AN ARCH OF BAMBOOS.

over channels of huge rocks and through scenes of almost majestic beauty; to the stretches of vivid greenery from Hunasgeria peak; to the lovely Matale hills, and the whole surrounding country viewed from the steep acclivities which embrace the town itself.

The climate of Kandy, considering its proximity to the equator, is surprisingly mild. A blanket at night is most welcome and comfortable, whereas in Colombo it is never required. The days are hot and glaring, but the refreshing early mornings and evenings admit of a goodly amount of vigorous exercise. Hotel accommodation is good, as it should be, where not a week passes without scores of fresh visitors from every part of the world. They come here to see the home of the later Singhalese Kings; the famous stronghold that was the last part of Ceylon to fall into the hands of foreigners; the Daladá Máligáwa, or Temple of the Sacred Tooth of Buddha; the lovely situation of the city; the most beautiful walks in the tropics; and the magnificent botanic gardens at Peradeniya.

Kandy is altogether a very attractive little place, and no wonder that passengers to all countries whose ships call for a day or two at the port of Colombo flock thither. We chiefly depend on our illustrations to give a correct idea of its scenery, but we must in words refer to some of the more notable features. The roads are bordered with fine trees and shrubs, and the frequent openings in the luxuriant foliage form exquisite framework through which we see the distant landscape as we wind about the hillsides. The avenues are as varied as they are beautiful. Here we are passing beneath an arch of bamboos which spread their feathery fronds from either side until they meet: there the grateful shade is bestowed by the huge broad leaves of the plantain that grow in profusion everywhere. These plants reach the height of twenty feet. The fruit (generally known in Europe as the banana) is so familiar all over the world that it needs no description. We may, however, remark that each plant after about a year's growth will probably bear about three hundred fruits weighing above sixty pounds; and it will then die exhausted by its bounteous effort.

Fruit and flowers of forms quite strange to the visitor grow in profusion everywhere, impressing one with the idea of luxury and plenty. We feel, as we roam along these luxurious paths, how happy and contented the people must be who live amidst such surroundings; and we reflect upon the contrast which it all bears to the barbarian and poverty-stricken Kandy under the tyrant kings, when the food of the people chiefly consisted of bark and roots, and their homes were squalid beyond conception. Such a transformation as this influx of wealth and comfort under British rule must be a convincing proof to the intelligent natives that their citadel at length fell to worthy conquerors, and a matter of proud satisfaction to every Englishman who reflects on the result of the enterprise.

The visitor who arrives at Kandy in the evening will probably be attracted to an after-dinner stroll around the lake, by the lower road, upon the banks. The first impressions gained amidst the buzz of myriads of winged insects, and the weird effect of the overhanging hillsides, sparkling with the fairy lights of fireflies, will not be easily forgotten. At

THE BROAD LEAVES OF THE PLANTAIN.

THE QUEEN'S HOTEL, KANDY, FROM THE UPPER LAKE ROAD.

a thousand points through the darkening foliage these wonderful little spirit-lights appear and disappear. Moonlight effects of purely tropical scenery are to be seen to perfection here, where the bold fronds of the palms, the traveller's tree, and the plantains stand in black relief at various elevations in the soft white light.

But the early riser will delight more in the effects of dawn, from the more elevated walks and drives. Two roads encircle the lake—the lower one at the water's edge, and the upper one at a high elevation on the hillsides. We choose the latter, and no sooner have we ascended to a moderate height, than a series of beautiful landscapes is presented to us through openings in the shrubs and trees which border the road. As we wind about the varied curves, the ever-changing aspect of the town and surrounding country presents a constant difference of outline and colour which is most enchanting.

By far the most interesting walk or drive in Kandy is that known as Lady Horton's, from which a distant view of the road just described can be obtained. Here we take our stand for a few moments and gaze across the lake at the tea estates upon the opposing slopes. There we notice a rugged cliff rising to the height of four thousand one hundred and nineteen feet. This is the highest point of the tea-growing district known as Hantanne. The estate upon this lofty eminence is called Hantanne estate; it comprises about 300 acres of tea, about 100 of cinchona, and about 600 of uncultivated forest and jungle. The adjoining estate, called Oodewelle, is the largest property of the district, and out of a total of 1,181 acres has 817 planted with tea. The total extent of the Hantanne district is 12,043 acres, divided into about 50 estates. The names of some of these have a familiar sound, such as Richmond Hill, Mount Pleasant, Primrose Hill, Hopewell, Fairieland, while others are most foreign to English ears, as Gontawalatenne, Doonoomadolawa, and Mapanawatura

One thing in connection with the names of estates strikes the stranger as most curious: the fact that every estate has two names, by one of which only it is known to the coolie labourers and by the other to Europeans. So that if you are making your way to Hopewell estate, and ask a coolie—even one who belongs to it—to direct you to Hopewell he will not know where it is; but if you ask for Anthonimally you will be taken direct to the estate which you know as Hopewell.

Although tea is the chief product of the Hantanne district, it is by no means the only one. Many of these acres are planted with cardamoms, pepper, cinchona, cacao, nutmegs, and there is even some coffee remaining as a memento of the old days when that product was king

The uncultivated hill on the left of Hantanne is a point of vantage where magnificent stretches of country may be seen. It is commonly known as "Mutton Button," a corruption of its correct name "Mattanapatana." The ascent of this hill, which is about 3,200 feet high, is a somewhat arduous task, and occupies from two to three hours; but our exertions are well rewarded by the splendid views which it commands.

We are still surveying the prospect from Lady

Horton's walk. So far our attention has been directed to the heights of Hantanne and "Mutton Button." We now turn a little to the right and through a fairy-like frame of feathery bamboos we look over the Government House Garden and the Christian Church of S. Paul in the direction of the famous Peradeniya Gardens, which we shall presently describe. On the right we see Primrose Hill, to which we have already referred as one of the Tea

FAIRY-LIKE FRAME OF FEATHERY BAMBOOS.

Estates of the Hantanne district. It will repay us for a few minutes to descend at this point to the grounds of "the Pavilion," one of the residences of the Governor of the Colony. This house was thus referred to by Sir Emerson Tennent in his work published about forty-five years ago: "In a park at the foot of this acclivity is the Pavilion of the Governor, one of the most agreeable edifices in India, not less for the beauty of its architecture than for its judicious adaptation to the climate.

The walls and columns are covered with chunam, prepared from calcined shells, which in whiteness and polish rivals the purity of marble. The high ground immediately behind is included in the demesne, and so successfully have the elegancies of landscape gardening been combined with the wildness of nature, that during my last residence in Kandy a leopard from the forest above came down nightly to drink at the fountain in the parterre."

THE PAVILION AT KANDY.

The house and grounds are still the same. Noble trees and ornamental plants abound everywhere and wild nature is still combined with effective artificial arrangement. Fine specimens of the Traveller's Tree are very noticeable here. This tree is so called from the useful function which the leaves display in sending forth a copious supply of water when pierced at the part where they burst forth from the stem. Nor are the trees and shrubs the only features of interest in this delightful garden; the creatures that appear everywhere lend their aid to charm the naturalist: geckoes, bloodsuckers, chameleons, lovely bright green lizards, about a foot in length, which, if interfered with, turn quite yellow in body, while the head becomes bright red; glorious large butterflies, with most lustrous wings; blue, green and scarlet dragon-flies of immense size; fascinating birds, giving life and colour to the scene; millepedes are amongst the creatures constantly crawling about; they are about a foot long, as thick as one's thumb, of a very glossy jet black colour, and possessed of about one hundred bright yellow legs. The strangest insects, too, are seen amongst the shrubs, so near akin to plant life that it is impossible to believe them to be alive until they are seen to move.

At the north-eastern point of the hill which rises behind the Pavilion the splendid Dumbara valley bursts into view. In spite of the clearings made for the cultivation of various products, it is still beautifully wooded. The lovely jungle is, however, fast giving way to the less beautiful but more wealth-creating tea and cocoa plantations. This district is about 12,000 acres in extent, about 7,000 of which are now under cultivation. The elevation, which is from 700 to 1,200 feet above sea level, is found to be most suitable for the cultivation of a large variety of products, especially when, as is the case with Dumbara, the rainfall is moderate and well distributed, being about 60 inches in the year. Such districts afford the planter an opportunity to adopt the wise course of carrying his eggs in more than one basket, whereas some districts will grow nothing but tea in sufficient abundance to be profitable. We see, therefore, in Dumbara, fields of cacao or chocolate trees with large rubber trees planted amongst them for shade. Some estates consist of fields of pepper, arecanuts, cocoanuts, cacao and coffee, while here and there are fields of tea bushes interspersed with cocoanuts. Vanilla and cardamoms are also represented. The district is, however, chiefly noted for its cacao or chocolate, of which it

A CACAO GROVE.

has about 5,000 acres. This fruit has been systematically cultivated in Ceylon only in quite recent times, and its introduction here was due to the necessity of introducing new products in the place of coffee about twenty years ago. In 1878 there were only 300 acres of cacao in the whole of Ceylon and the export for the year was but little more than one thousand pounds. Now there are twenty-one thousand acres and the export last year amounted to nearly six million lbs. realising about £300,000.

Beyond the Dumbara valley we notice in the far distance the outline of a noble mountain which is known as the Knuckles. The top of this mountain is shaped by four distinct elevations resembling the knuckles of the hand, from which circumstance its name is derived. It is an important district under cultivation for tea, cinchona, cardamoms, and other products. The estates opened up extend to more than eight thousand acres. Its elevation varies from 3,000 to 6,000 feet.

We will now descend from the lofty pedestal where we have seen spread out before us the beautiful Kandyan district and by way of diversion pay a visit to the principal characteristic building of the town known as the Daladá Máligáwa or Temple of the Tooth. Our picture commemorates the occasion of the visit of the Crown Prince of Austria in 1893. The crowd had assembled to witness the arrival of His Royal Highness at the temple where he was about to inspect the sacred tooth of Buddha. This revered relic is shown only on very special occasions. Before we accompany His Royal Highness to the scene within, one or two features of the exterior are worthy of remark.

The temporary erection in front of the main entrance is an arch of welcome. It is a structure known in Ceylon as the Pandal. In the construction of this form of decoration the Singhalese excel to a surprising degree, so much so that I do not hesitate to assert that in no other country is such effective decoration by means of foliage, fruit and flowers, on occasions of festivity, ever to be seen. It is true that they practise the art on every possible occasion, and thereby they naturally become proficient in an occupation so much to their taste. Every wedding, silver wedding and golden, is celebrated by a lavish display of Pandals, and every distinguished guest is welcomed in the same gay and effective manner, the decorations often being on a very extensive scale. A Singhalese Pandal is never heavy but is always elegant. The materials are entwined on a shapely and artistic framework of bamboo, which is sometimes attached to complete stems of the beautiful areca palm, forming columns on either side, and consist of plumes from the finest palms, trails of beautiful climbing ferns, lovely mosses, bright blossoms of great beauty, almost every kind of tropical fruit and flowers, green oranges, golden oranges, pineapples, palmyra nuts, cocoanuts, kitul berries, and many more kinds of less familiar fruits.

The Temple and the Pattirippuwa, which is the name of the octagonal building on the right of the main entrance, are enclosed by a very ornamental stone wall and a moat. The Temple itself is concealed by the other buildings within the enclosure. Upon entering we pass through a small quadrangle and turn to the right up a flight of stone steps to the Temple itself. The most noticeable features are grotesque carvings, highly-coloured frescoes, representing torments in store for various classes of sinners, and images of Buddha. A most torturous noise is kept up by tom-tom beating, and the sound of various native instruments. On either side are flower sellers, and the atmosphere is heavy with perfume of the lovely white blossoms. Each worshipper in the Temple brings an offering of some fragrant flower.

THE DALADÁ MÁLIGÁWA AT KANDY.

The beautiful Plumiera, with its pure creamy petals and yellow heart, is the most popular sacrificial blossom, and this, together with jasmine and oleander, is everywhere strewn by devout Singhalese. The numbers of yellow-robed priests, the Kandyan chiefs in their rich white and gold dresses and curious jewel-bespangled hats, and the various richly-coloured costumes of the crowds of reverent worshippers of both sexes, form a scene striking in the extreme. The Kandyan chiefs had assembled on this occasion in considerable force, and were a very distinctive feature of the scene. They are naturally handsome men, and when attired, as they were, in full court dress, they look very imposing. To begin with, they contrive to wind about their persons some one hundred and fifty yards of fine silk or muslin, embroidered in gold, in form to render themselves somewhat of the shape of a peg-top. This drapery, tapered finely down to the ankles, ends in neat little frills. Round the waist is fastened a velvet gold-embroidered belt. Over a shirt, fastened with magnificent jewelled studs, they wear a jacket with very full sleeves, fastened tight above the elbow, and made of brightest coloured brocaded silks. Their hats are of very curious shape, even more gorgeously embroidered than the jackets, and studded with jewels.

We enter a narrow doorway and notice two pairs of elephants' tusks on either side, and some very curious metal work on the door itself; this leads to a steep narrow staircase, at the end of which is a door most elaborately inlaid with silver and ivory; through this we enter the little sanctuary which contains the jealously-guarded sacred tooth, the palladium of Ceylon, and an object of unbounded reverence to four hundred millions of people. Within this chamber, in dim religious light, we notice a solid silver table, behind which the huge silver-gilt Dagoba, or bell-shaped shrine, with six inner shrines protecting the tooth, is usually visible through thick metal bars. But to-day the visit of the Crown Prince of Austria is honoured by an unlocking of the bolts and bars, the nest of priceless shrines is brought forward, and the tooth is displayed, upheld by a twist of golden wire, from the heart of the large golden lotus blossom. The shrines, however, attract our notice much more than the supposed tooth of Gautama Buddha. They are all of pure gold, ornamented with magnificent rubies, pearls, emeralds, and catseyes, the last two being quite covered with rubies. Besides these treasures we see many priceless offerings and gifts of kings, including an image of Buddha carved out of one gigantic emerald, about three inches long by two deep. There were also many chains set with precious stones and other ornaments.

We are glad soon to retreat from this small chamber, so hot, and filled with almost overpowering perfume of the Plumiera blossoms, and to visit the Oriental Library in the Octagon. In the balcony we pause awhile and become refreshed as we look around upon the motley crowd below. The chief priest with great courtesy now shows us a very rare and valuable collection of manuscripts of great antiquity. Most of them are in Pàli and Sanskrit characters, not written but pricked with a stylus on narrow strips of palm leaf about three inches wide and sixteen or twenty inches long. These strips form the leaves of the books, and are strung together between two boards which form the covers. Many of the covers are ornamented elaborately with embossed metal, and some are even set with jewels. Besides the sacred and historical writings, there are works on astronomy, mathematics and other subjects.

Some account of the customs of the natives will naturally be looked for in these pages, and here we

ONE OF THE TEMPLE STUD.

may refer to one called the Perahara, which is connected with this Temple of the Tooth. It is a night procession of pre-historic origin and forms one of the most weird sights to be seen in this or any other country. Attached to the temple is a stud of some forty fine elephants which, when not in use for festival purposes, are kept on the estates of the native chiefs in the district. These elephants are brought into the grounds and a night procession of the following description takes place. The route, a large quadrangle in front of the Temple, was illuminated by torches and small lanterns placed in niches purposely constructed for them in the ornamental walls. The finest elephant was taken into the temple by the main entrance, visible in our picture on page 71, and caparisoned with gorgeous trappings quite covering his huge head and body, the face-covering being richly embroidered in gold, silver, and jewels, and surmounted with an image of Buddha; the tusks also encased in splendid sheaths. The shrine of the tooth is removed and placed within the howdah, the whole being surmounted by a huge canopy supported by rods which are held on either side by natives. Two lesser elephants are now brought up and decorated in a somewhat similar manner, and are then placed to escort the great elephant, one on each side. Several headmen now mount the elephants, holding baskets of flowers, and their attendants sit behind, holding gold and silver umbrellas. The other elephants are then brought up into procession, all mounted in a similar way by headmen and their attendants. Between each section are rows of other headmen in gorgeous dresses, and groups of masked devil-dancers in the most barbaric costumes, dancing frantically, adopting every possible contortion, and producing the most hideous noise by the beating of tom-toms, blowing of conch-shells; the clanging of brass cymbals, the blowing of shrill pipes and other instruments useful in creating the most ear-splitting devil-music that can be imagined. Nothing more eerie can be imagined than this procession, about a mile long, consisting of thousands of dark brown figures, gaily dressed, intermingling with hideous groups of devil-dancers, all frantically gesticulating around the forty elephants by the dim red light of a thousand torches. It seems extraordinary that under the present conditions of fast-increasing civilisation among them that they should carry out such festivities with real barbaric zeal; but they seem to do so, and as the Perahara has continued to be celebrated for twenty-five centuries it is not safe to predict its discontinuance.

A KANDYAN VILLAGE.

CHAPTER VI.

PERADENIYA GARDENS.

BEFORE we proceed on further quest of planting enterprise we must visit an institution near Kandy which is intimately connected with the agricultural prosperity of the country—the Peradeniya Gardens. Here agricultural possibilities are put to the test and experimental culture is carried on in order to discover products likely to increase the wealth of the colony. Especially is it of value to the native agriculturist; for it supplies him with seeds, advice, and instruction free of cost. A paternal government cares for his prosperity; finds out what it is advisable for him to grow, and experiments upon the product for him; advises him upon every point, and periodically inquires how he is getting on. The curator of the gardens, always a distinguished scientific botanist, has under him a talented staff, and presides over the whole department of experimental culture, including gardens in other parts of the country. I shall not weary my readers with details of the experiments made here with cacao and other products, or with any attempt to describe the various departments of culture to be found at Peradeniya, where the whole flora of the island is represented;

but a short description of the gardens will, I venture to think, be welcome. The situation is four miles from Kandy, where the great sandy river, the Mahaweli-ganga, assumes a horse-shoe curve almost enclosing the gardens; and it is here that the botanic splendour in which Ceylon is so richly clothed from shore to shore undoubtedly reaches its highest point of magnificence.

Before passing into this stately enclosure we are attracted by a fine avenue of india-rubber trees (*ficus elastica*) near the entrance. The little plant, with bright green oval leaves, which in England we are accustomed to see in sitting-rooms and conservatories, grows in its native land to an enormous size, and throws out horizontal boughs to an extent of more than fifty feet. It is most remarkable, however, for its snake-like roots, which extend from the base of the trunk to a wider extent than the height of the tree. Sometimes they reach out more than one hundred feet, and in appearance they resemble huge pythons crawling over the surface of the soil. That portion of the root which rises above the surface occasionally reaches to such a height that a tall man can stand upright behind it and yet be hidden; it is not cylindrical, but flattened, so that it really resembles a wall. When these noble trees are wounded, tears trickle down their stems, and harden into the india-rubber of commerce. A double row of these giants form a magnificent avenue just outside the gardens. The great boughs are interlaced, and their silvery stems so shaped that they appear to be writhing each in another's toils. They are indeed a stately sight, forming a worthy approach to the wonders beyond them.

The Royal Botanic Gardens were established very soon after the occupation of the Kandyan kingdom by the English. All European ideas of a garden must be dispelled if we wish to realise the general features of Peradeniya. There is an entire absence of formal arrangement, but the beautifully undulated land of about one hundred and fifty acres presents a grand effect—a garden and park combined, under the most favourable conditions for both. Dr. Trimen, the late accomplished director of the gardens, remarks that "here nature asserts herself almost uncontrolled; she gives us grandeur of form, wealth of foliage, exuberance of growth, and splendour of colour—unfading beauties, but of a quite different kind from those of the sweet summer flower-gardens or the well-kept stoves and greenhouses of England." Of course scientific instruction is the primary object of the gardens, but still picturesque effect must have been studied with great care in planting the groups of trees and arranging the various families of plants. Upon entering the gardens such magnificent groups of palms greet us that we halt in amazement. A specimen of each one indigenous to the island, in company with many noble specimens of foreign lands, are seen in massive assemblage, wreathed with flowering creepers, and bearing on their trunks lovely sprays of elegant ferns. At the end of the entrance avenue one of these stately groups is surrounded by a beautiful parterre, displaying many of the most notable flowering shrubs. On the left of the entrance, which itself is draped with a graceful creeper, the Bignonia Unguis-cati of Brazil, is a wall covered with dense masses of the Burmese Thunbergia

THE SCREW PINE

creeper, with lovely bell-shaped blossoms of pale violet-blue, and many fine old tree trunks, clothed in the same beautiful manner. Near this spot are to be seen gamboge trees, and some very curious African trees, with long pendulous fruits. Continuing in the same direction, we come to a charming little pool, which is seen to the best advantage at seven o'clock in the morning, when the reflection of the bamboos and the palms upon its banks is so perfect that, save for the narrow strips of leaf on the surface of the water, the view presented in the pool is as exact in all detail as the real one.

To the south of the pool will be noticed some giant clumps of Malacca Bamboo, in diameter about nine inches, and reaching to a height of one hundred feet. During the rains they may almost be seen to grow, so rapidly do they increase their height and bulk. I cannot say what is the fullest extent to which they increase in a single day, but one foot is somewhere near the minimum during the heavy rainfall in June and July.

As we approach the pretty corner at the extreme south of the gardens, which is represented by our illustration entitled *The Screw Pine*, the noticeable features are varieties of succulent plants in a pretty rockery, especially the *Boucerosia umbellata*, with purple velvet flowers, a miniature plantation of chocolate trees of various kinds, india-rubber trees, gutta-percha trees, a large number of beds of pretty flowers, and many young palms recently planted out. The drive at this end of the garden forms a loop, around which are screw pines, agaves, aloes, and bamboos. The Screw Pine (*Pandanus*), with its scarlet-orange fruits, tempting only to monkeys, its sword-like glossy leaves, its forked cylindrical stem so beautifully chased, and its strange stilt-like roots, presents a most fantastic appearance.

In our illustration may be seen a portion of the bridge over the Mahaweli-ganga, which, as we have observed, almost embraces the whole garden. The high banks are in many parts clothed with climbing shrubs between the enormous thickets of bamboo, which wave their plumes over river and path. And these huge clumps of eighty or a hundred cylindrical stems rising to such a lofty height are really bunches of grass! Their stems are knotted like all grasses, of which they are the most wonderful species. They grow closely crowded together from a common root.

Peradeniya is so full of marvels that I find it difficult to select any for brief notice. No book descriptive of Ceylon should, however, omit mention of the Talipot Palm. Here is a specimen of a young tree. This majestic palm for the first ten years grows only magnificent, fan-shaped leaves, as seen in our photograph; next a trunk begins to form, which grows straight as a mast to a height of about one hundred feet. It is a grand white stem encircled with closely set ring-marks, where it has borne and shed its leaves from year to year. The semi-circular fans are often as large as fifteen feet in radius, giving a surface of about one hundred and fifty square feet. The uses to which they are put are computed by the natives at eight hundred and one, the foremost of these being rain-cloak and sunshade. Three or four of these leaves form an admirable tent, and are often used as such. The literary use to which they have for thousands of years been applied is perhaps the most interesting. For this they are cut into strips, and afterwards boiled and dried, when they form what the natives term *ola* or paper. On strips of *ola* the history and the religious codes of the people have been handed down to us. I have seen manuscripts of this description more than two thousand years old, and yet in beautiful condition,

THE YOUNG TALIPOT

with the Páli characters so clear and distinct that it is difficult to realise their vast age.

When the Talipot attains full maturity, it grows somewhat smaller leaves, and develops a gigantic bud some four feet in height. In due course it bursts with a report, and a lovely white blossom unfolds itself, and spreads into a majestic pyramid of cream-coloured flowers, which rise to a height of twenty feet above the leafy crown. The fruit which follows on this magnificent blossoming consists of innumerable nuts, which, however, are useless. Their appearance is a sign that the noble tree is near its end. It now begins to droop, its magnificent leaves wither, and within a year it falls dead. In our little picture below will be seen a Talipot Palm in flower. Here, in the Kandyan district beautiful palms of many species flourish amongst the tea, lending the quality of picturesqueness to

PALMS AMONGST THE TEA.

fields which would otherwise appear monotonous. Robert Knox's quaint description of the Talipot is worth quoting. He says :—

"It is as big and tall as a ship's mast, and very straight, bearing only leaves which are of great use and benefit to this people, one single leaf being so broad and large that it will cover some fifteen or twenty men, and keep them dry when it rains. The leaf being dried is very strong and limber, and most wonderfully made for men's convenience to carry along with them, for though this leaf be thus broad when it is open, yet it will fold close like a lady's fan, and then it is no bigger than a man's arm. It is wonderfully light; they cut them into pieces and carry them in their hands. The whole leaf-spread is round almost like a circle, but being cut in pieces for use are near like unto a triangle; they lay them upon their heads as they travel, with the peaked end foremost, which is convenient to make their way through the boughs and thickets. When the sun is vehement hot they use them to shade themselves from the heat; soldiers all carry them, for besides the benefit of keeping them dry in case it rain upon the march, these leaves make their tents to lie under in the night. A marvellous mercy, which Almighty God hath bestowed upon this poor and naked people in this rainy country."*

The fernery is one of the most beautiful spots in the garden, and has been planned with excellent taste. Beneath the shade of lofty trees pretty rivulets flow between banks carpeted with ferns of every kind, some so minute as to be hardly distinguishable from delicate moss, others robust and tree-like, and some even bearing fine tufts of feathery leaves as large as stately palms. Climbing ferns and many pretty parasites cover the trunks of the huge trees which protect the shade-loving plants beneath them. The presence of many most gorgeous butterflies flitting around adds much to the fairy-like beauty of the scene. Some parts of the

---

* Raja Singha II., King of Kandy in 1660-1680, had an extraordinary passion for detaining white men as prisoners in his dominions. Robert Knox, who wrote an admirable account of Kandy in the reign of Charles II., was kidnapped at Trincomali. See chapter on Trincomali.

garden are left to nature, and the trees and plants are self-grown. Their wild luxuriance, however, has to be kept in check.

A list of the most interesting trees and plants, or even some reference to each of the walks and drives, without illustrations would be wearisome. Suffice it to say, therefore, that in Peradeniya gardens will be found the most lavish display of tropical flora that can possibly be conceived; for here are brought together beautiful representatives of every species. Seeds, plants, and cuttings are supplied to every part of the island, and a great deal of experimental culture is carried on in order to discover products likely to increase the wealth of the colony, so that the practical benefit of such a garden is manifest.

As we are interesting ourselves in the people as well as their beautiful country, we will stroll into the pretty village which nestles under the palms and bamboos at a corner of the gardens on the left of the entrance. It is approached by way of a satin-wood bridge, which spans the Mahaweli-ganga. This bridge is a remarkable structure; it spans the river with a single arch, in which there is neither nail nor bolt, the whole of the massive wood-work being merely dovetailed together. It is constructed entirely of beautiful yellow satinwood, which fifty years ago was so plentiful in the forests of Ceylon that it was used for common building purposes. This wood is extremely hard and durable, as is evidenced by the present condition of the bridge, which has now withstood the effects of excessive damp and tropical heat for sixty-two years without visible deterioration. Under normal conditions the river flows fully seventy feet below the arch, but at the burst of the monsoon such a mighty torrent rolls between these lovely bamboo-fringed banks that the bridge then clears the water by about ten feet only.

The river here flows between the garden and the village. Immediately upon crossing the bridge we come upon typical scenes of village life. Our picture

NATIVE HUT AT PERADENIYA.

shows much that is characteristic of every Singhalese village; the native women, with a large red chattie, made of porous earthenware, placed upon her hip; the domesticated buffalo; the temporary Buddhist shrine, erected to receive the offerings of devout way-farers—it will be noticed that this modest erection consists of a chair surmounted by a framework of bamboo sticks, covered by a few strips of calico, forming a canopy within which is placed a small image of Buddha and a bowl for offerings; at the close of the day the offerings are conveyed to the Temple of the Tooth at Kandy. The native hut which does duty as a dwelling-house and refreshment stall is quite representative. Its walls and floor are of mud, its roof of the dried fronds of palm leaves, and the front is opened or closed by means of wooden planks. The usual swarm of little brown urchins frolic on the roadside, and add not a little to the picturesqueness of the scene. Beside the hut tower palms to the height of ninety feet, waving their glorious crowns above a luxuriant undergrowth of smaller trees, shrubs, and flowering creepers; and in the lovely little wild gardens grow pepper, curry seeds, garlic, pumpkins, sweet potatoes—all in wild profusion.

Not many yards farther on we notice that the native huts are embowered by bread-fruit trees, the foliage of which is in marked contrast with the waving plumes of the cocoanut and other palms amongst which it grows. The fruit, which is very abundant, grows in large green pods, about the size of melons, which nestle beneath each separate crown of leaves. It is used as food by the natives in various preparations, but is, as a rule, disliked by Europeans.

Here is the perfection of village life; the people lay themselves down to rest upon their palm-leaf mats, spread upon the bare ground, with the palm-thatch above them, happy and peaceful in the knowledge that over and around them grows an abundant supply of all their needs, while the same beneficent climate which is the efficient cause of such bountiful means of nourishment provides warmth without clothing, and renders their "wants but little here below." They need no poor laws, nor have they any. Poverty is relieved by the natural

CONTENT WITH NATURE'S GIFTS.

benevolence of the people. The wealthy Singhalese are especially kind to the poor, and many of them have fixed days of the week upon which they distribute rice to all the aged and infirm of their district. The solidarity of the family is, I believe, even stronger among them than Europeans; the weakest are the most cared for; the rich help their poorer relations, and never disown them; the poor assist the poorer amongst their own relatives and friends, so that there is no dread of old age poverty. In these particulars of freedom from care and squalid misery I believe that the Singhalese are now the happiest of Her Majesty's subjects in any part of the world.

Indeed the wants of the Singhalese are very few; they live in great contentment, with apparently no ambition to possess more than a modest little hut, furnished only with a few palm-leaf plaited mats, on which habit enables them to enjoy perfect repose; the streams which abound everywhere provide them with baths, which are their chief luxury, and in which their naturally cleanly habits cause them to take great pleasure. They are to be found at all hours of the day combing and drying their long black hair on the banks, after which process they renew its gloss with cocoanut oil and twist it into a coil. Nature is their kindly mother, and supplies them with every gift which their gentle and subdued dispositions need. Hurry and bustle, so characteristic of the advancement of Western civilisation, is unknown to them. Even in the bazaars of the large towns, all rush and confusion, such as one sees in the markets of continental towns of Southern Europe, is entirely absent. The noiseless tread of their bare feet, and their dilatory movements, are in great contrast to anything like tumult, although the scene is never quiet, for they are great talkers, and use their voices at a high pitch. Fortunately, the Singhalese language is beautifully soft in sound, even more so than Italian. A curious circumstance connected with their great loquaciousness is that the vocabulary of the poorer classes is exceedingly

THE GRAM VENDOR

small. I have heard it stated that some of the coolie class understand only some three hundred words, and in their conversation use fewer.

A familiar character is the roadside gram vendor. There is always one to be seen near Peradeniya Bridge. She sits patiently during the greater part of the day selling grain by the half-centsworth to passers-by. As might be conjectured from the size of the little bamboo measure, this grain is being sold in very small quantities as a luxury. It resembles dried peas, and tastes rather like them.

CHAPTER VII.

MÁTALÉ.

IT will now be found convenient to visit Mátalé, the most northerly district cultivated by Europeans, and at present the utmost point to which the railway extends in this direction. But we prefer to proceed thither by road; for we do not wish to move rapidly through the beautiful scenery of the Kandyan country. A glimpse of the way is shown in our picture.

THE ROAD FROM KANDY TO MÁTALË.

The drive of seventeen miles is a very interesting one, and easy with the exception of the steep descent of three or four miles just before the town of Mátalé is reached. Upon arrival here we find a comfortable rest-house fitted with every convenience for the traveller and well provisioned. Bath and breakfast are the first consideration, after which we walk leisurely through the town, which contains one of the largest purely native bazaars in Ceylon, extending for almost a mile in one long street shaded by a fine avenue of rain trees, so called from the circumstance that at night the leaves fold into a kind of sack in which the moisture condenses, and at sunrise when the leaves open is discharged in quite a shower. Here are to be seen the necessaries and luxuries for the supply of the native community throughout the large and important planting district of which Mátalé is the centre. All the shops are after the fashion of open stalls, and the traders, their goods and transactions, from one end of the street to the other, are open to the gaze of passers-by. The barber, the tinker, the merchant of gay-coloured cloths, and the curry-stuff vendor, are all doing a roaring trade. The mellifluous tones of Ramasamy's voice are unceasing, and the stranger will not fail to be struck with surprise at the inordinate amount of talking required by every trifling bargain. Some quaint workshops are to be found here. Ivory carving, and the elaborate chasing of ceremonial swords, such as were worn at the Kandyan state ceremonies, and are still part of the official uniform of native chiefs holding office under the British Government, are still executed here. There is also a very pretty and delicate industry carried on in the weaving of grass matting for the covering of couches and chairs. Mátalé is not without its antiquarian interest also. Here it was that about 100 B.C. in the famous cave of Aluwihari the Buddhist codes

THE MÁTALÉ ROAD BLOCKED BY ELEPHANTS.

SCENERY OF THE MÁTALÉ DISTRICT.

of religion, which had previously been preserved only by tradition, were inscribed upon palm leaves, and thus preserved to future generations. The scenery has the same characteristics as the Kandyan district, and is especially beautiful in its wealth and variety of tropical foliage. The hills, visible in our picture, rise to an altitude of five thousand feet, and are wooded to the summits, save where clearings have been made for the cultivation of coffee, cacao,

CARTING PRODUCE TO MÁTALÉ RAILWAY STATION.

and tea; they exhibit fine specimens of some of the most remarkable trees in Ceylon, including many iron-wood trees, with crimson-tipped foliage and delicate flowers. Mátalé, being a very extensive district, has three divisions, north, east, and west. The northern division reaches to Nalanda, the first coaching stage on the main road to the famous ruined city of Anuradhapura. The eastern and western divisions are right and left of this road, so that the large number of visitors who now journey to the ruined cities pass through the heart of this district and see the fine tea and cacao estates for which it is famous. The total extent of estates is about sixty thousand acres, of which nearly half is cultivated. The elevation being from 1,200 to 4,000 feet, mixed planting is popular; and we find, in addition to tea and cacao, cardamoms, cocoanuts, arecanuts, annatto, kola, rubber, cinchona, vanilla, pepper, sapan, and

PEPPER GROVE IN THE MATALÉ DISTRICT.

sago. There are thousands of acres of rich forest which contains much ebony, satinwood, halmilla, and palu.

Of climate, scenery, and products Mátalé affords great variety. It has its lowlands, with their cocoanut, vanilla and cocoa groves, and the warm glow of tropical sunshine; hills of moderate elevation, in some parts cultivated, in others wild and forest-clad; lofty mountains, with their cool and invigorating atmosphere so inviting to Europeans; and it stretches away to the north in spurs which gradually decrease amidst a vast wilderness of forest and scrub, the haunt of the elephant, leopard, buffalo and bear. Big game is to be found in proximity to estates, and is still more plentiful a day's march to the north. Sambur, barking deer, and pig afford good hunting; while the leopard, bear, and buffalo are available as victims for the sportsman's gun. Few planting

A RELIEF TO THE MONOTONOUS LITTLE TEA BUSHES.

districts can boast of sporting grounds so good and accessible.

CHAPTER VIII.

MÁTALÉ TO RAMBODDE.

WE must now retrace our journey as far as Peradeniya, and thence we shall pass over new ground, in a southward direction, through the very heart of the greatest tea districts of this tea-growing land. We shall not, however, proceed far before crying halt, as far as the railway is concerned. First we pass

"A FERTILE AND BEAUTIFUL VALLEY."

through a fertile and beautiful valley. Here the chief attraction lies in a series of rice fields, where the mud-enamoured buffalo is seen harnessed to the primitive plough, the classic implement of Virgil's Italy. We marvel at his strength in turning a furrow of full eighteen inches in these fields of mud.

Pass when we will, at any season of the year, the domestic buffalo is always a prominent figure in the landscape. He may be treading out rice on the threshing-floor, as heedless of the muzzle as though he were a subject of the Mosaic law, or wallowing idly in the most miry place he can find, but he will always be there. Although so quiet and useful when tamed and broken in, he is the same species as the dangerous beast that affords such exciting sport in the jungle, where he is an enemy by no means to be despised. Those heavy ribbed horns which lie apparently so harmless on his shoulders are good both for attack and defence, and when threatened

PLOUGHING RICE FIELDS.

either by man or beast he is a very dangerous and resolute antagonist. It will be admitted that rice cultivation, though not the cleanest or most pleasant of occupations, is suited to a slim and wiry race like the Singhalese, the paucity of whose clothing is not without obvious advantages. The appearance of the fields is very interesting, whether seen in the flooded stage, when the terraces on the hill-sides are converted into tiny lakes of fantastic shapes, or when the same terraces, tier above tier, are waving with ripening corn.

At the eighth mile from Peradeniya we reach the town of Gampola, for a time the seat of Singhalese power. As the last of the native capitals of Ceylon before the removal of the moribund dynasty to Cotta in 1410, Gampola can claim to be a place of considerable interest. Moreover, it is the point at which the roads of several important tea districts converge; and it is this circumstance that causes us to alight.

Here, on the east of the railway as we are proceeding southwards, stretch some of the districts that were the earliest in the mountains to be stripped of their virgin forest by the European. To the west lies the picturesque district of Dolosbage, which lends itself admirably to pictorial treatment; but with so many claiming our attention we must of necessity leave some with merely passing reference. Dolosbage is pre-eminently a tea district, there being scarcely any other product now under extensive cultivation. The estates, of which there are about seventy, vary in elevation from two to four thousand feet, and comprise about twenty-seven thousand acres, sixteen thousand of which are under cultivat on.

We prefer here to visit the districts of Pussellawa and Rambodde, which lie to the east of the railway, because they have more notable associations and are familiar to thousands who journeyed through them to the mountain sanatorium of Nuwara Eliya in the olden days, before the advent of the railway. The old town of Gampola is still the railway terminus for these districts, and from it an excellent macadamised road passes through Pussellawa, Rambodde, and over the heights of Nuwara Eliya, to descend again amongst the rolling patanas and deep glens of the Uva country, which we shall see later. This road scales the mountain slopes by zig-zag cuttings, now on the mountain-side, now passing through narrow defiles and onwards upon the verge of deep abysses,

RAMBODDE.

beautiful everywhere, in many parts enchanting, and in one—the pass above Rambodde—magnificent.

For the first stage—Gampola to Pussellawa—the luxuriant growth of tropical vegetation, which here seems to reach the height of its loveliness, and the torrents foaming in the ravines below the tortuous paths, present a singularly beautiful panorama.

The sensation of enchanting peace, and the pure

and invigorating atmosphere, which is so noticeable upon arriving at Pussellawa after a walk from the heated plains, once experienced will never be forgotten. Eight miles below, by the winding road, lies Gampola in almost insufferable heat, yet here one may rest beneath the shade of orange trees, laden with their golden fruit, and breathe such pure cool air as only those who have been for months in the enervating heat of the lowlands can fully

THE SENSATION OF ENCHANTING PEACE.

appreciate. When looking down upon the simmering haze which enshrouds the lower valleys, and glancing back at the cool blue shadows of the surrounding hills, fresh life creeps through the veins, and a feeling of supreme delight enthralls every sense. Here the gardens combine the characteristics of England and the tropics. Bright with lilacs, pinks, convolvuli, passion flowers, and crotons of every fantastic admixture of colour, they are no less gay with butterflies and birds of brightest plumage, while delicious fruits are plentiful around.

Pussellawa was notable in the old days of coffee for many pioneer efforts, and here fortunes were made and lost before the fine stretches of tea that we now see were planted.

From Pussellawa to Rambodde the road winds along the mountain side in picturesque contortions through the lovely vale of Kotmalee, where the

THE GLEN OF RAMBODDE.

Mahawelli-ganga rolls majestically down its mountain course, fed by numerous torrents from neighbouring ravines, till we come to the glen of Rambodde, which is one of the most romantic spots in the whole of Ceylon. At first sight it appears to be a sort of *cul de sac.* An apparently insurmountable barrier of mountains seems to defy the traveller who would reach the plain of Nuwara Eliya, 3,000 feet above. But the steep acclivities that bound the narrow gorge have been terraced with winding roads, by means of which the almost precipitous hill may be surmounted. The defile is entered between two of the finest cataracts in Ceylon, descending upon either side of the pass, the Puna-Ella and the Garunda-Ella, both tributaries of the Mahawelli-ganga, which they join in the valley below. From this point the ascent begins in real earnest, the gradient increasing to one in fourteen. The traveller on foot may save several miles by short-cut paths, but this alternative is literally mountain climbing, and entails a considerable amount of exertion. Before the cultivation of coffee caused such immense destruction of primæval forest on either side of this lovely gorge, the scenery must have been surprisingly beautiful.

By the first four miles of road above Rambodde we reach a further elevation of a thousand feet, and now we can sit in the delightful cool atmosphere and gaze upon the grand panorama of the Kotmalee valley, over thousands of acres of tea flourishing to perfection upon the slopes and rocky crags of the broken country, interspersed with dense masses of forest, glowing with every imaginable tint.

But grand and beautiful as are the prospects presented by day from the heights above Rambodde, they are surpassed by the scenes in the gorge below by night. The Moon, thrice as brilliant as in northern Europe, yet having a slight tinge of gold that gives a softness to her rays; the air, pure and cool, perfumed with the sweet fragrance of lemon grass; all nature silent, save the mighty tones of distant cataracts, and the music of mountain streams; tree ferns, wonderful in beauty and variety, exhibiting

THE RAMBODDE ROAD

TEA FIELDS IN THE RAMBODDE PASS.

every curve and pattern of their lovely fronds that fringe the silvery torrents which leap on both sides into the valley; the weird shadows of the dark rocks on the opposing slopes; the grand flow of outline along the ridges, centred in the distance by a lofty double cone—these are some of the features of a moonlight scene in the pass of Rambodde. But I am forgetting that it is now twenty-four years since I was a solitary witness of this scene, and that in more recent years the hill sides have been still further denuded of their beautiful forests to make way for the extension of tea cultivation; still the beauty of the district has not entirely disappeared, and even now many miles of the landscape are lovely beyond description.

Our illustrations here are very interesting as showing one of the earliest nurseries of Ceylon tea. It is a matter of history that in the forties the owners of Rothschild Estate in Pussellawa, the district through which we have just passed, planted some tea there, and that in later years they transferred some plants to the locality illustrated by us in the Rambodde pass. But tea-making was little understood, and the outlay for every pound prepared was about £5. The plants, however, continued to flourish; and the author remembers very well passing through these experimental gardens in the seventies, when they were looking splendid. At this time the Ceylon Company were in possession of the estate, and paid great attention to it, employing experienced tea-planters from India. But strange to say, considering ensuing events, they were unable to make it a commercial success, and instead of their efforts hastening the development of the industry, they for some time retarded it. Want of success in these early days was doubtless due to want of experience, but perseverance eventually overcame all difficulties, and improved systems of plucking, pruning, and manufacturing at length bore fruit in immensely increased crop returns and an improved quality of the product. The estates Condegalla and Labookellie, which we have chosen for illustration in the Rambodde Pass, were the scene of the early struggles; they are now

LABOOKELLIE.

most flourishing, and have passed from the old Ceylon Company to the Eastern Produce and Estates Company.

Pussellawa and Rambodde, which we have taken together, comprise estates to the extent of thirty-three thousand acres, about twenty thousand of which are under cultivation of tea, and the remainder are still forest and grass land. There is very little cinchona or coffee in these districts.

Although in visiting Labookellie we have approached to within seven miles of Nuwara Eliya, the famous mountain sanitarium to which considerable reference will be made later, we must now return to Gampola and thence proceed through the central and largest of all the tea districts.

PLUCKING TEA.

CHAPTER IX.

GAMPOLA TO HATTON.

GAMPOLA, to which we have already referred as a town with historical associations and as a station at which several districts converge, is itself on the southern borders of the planting district of Kadugannawa. Although we were about to pass this district unnoticed amongst so many we must pause for a moment. Immediately upon leaving Gampola station on our upward journey we pass by one of the most famous estates in Ceylon—Mariawatte, famous alike for its marvellous yield and the high quality of its tea. Here we are on the very spot where planting enterprise in Ceylon first began and where the first coffee estates were opened, as far back as 1824. It is curious to find one of the finest tea estates upon the site of an old abandoned coffee estate, but so it is; coffee failed where Mariawatte now yields her 1,000 lbs. of made tea from every acre year by year. It is interesting to note also that as this estate was one of the most successful, so it was one of the first planted with tea on a large scale. Moreover, the fortunate owners who made this wise move were not experienced planters but railway contractors. The same gentlemen also successfully pioneered in other districts, notably the Kelani Valley.

After leaving Gampola there is so much to see that the eye must be constantly on the alert. We are now about to pass through the Tea Estates of Ambagamuwa, the wettest planting district in Ceylon, having an annual rainfall of about 200 inches, or eight times that of London. We ascend in snake-like windings of every possible shape, now along the almost precipitous rock trimly cut like the scarp of a fortress, now right through masses of solid gneiss, and out into the open eminence again, the scene changing with every curve. At one point we come upon a sight especially interesting, but which will nevertheless elude all but the expectant traveller—the entrance and exit of the Hog's-back Tunnel. As we approach, the mountain is cleft by a deep narrow ravine, which is in reality a watercourse, down whose steeps rushes a torrent towards the river in the valley below. Over this the train passes, affording a grand spectacle when the water, in the south-west monsoon, dashes with resistless force amongst the boulders and broken crags of the chasm, above which the train seems momentarily suspended. The vision lasts but a few seconds, when the tunnel heightens the keen sense of wonderment with its contrast of absolute darkness. In a few moments more the scene seems to reappear as the mountain-side is cleft again, and an exactly similar ravine is bridged, followed by the darkness of a second tunnel. After obtaining a view of the Galbodda Cliff on the left we arrive at Galbodda station. Still we ascend in ever-winding course, and as we pass through Blackwater and Weweltalawa estates a grand open view is afforded extending over the low country right away to the famous Kelani Valley. Some idea of this scene will be gathered from our little picture below. Even Colombo is said to be discernible from this point on a clear day.

The Dickoya district with its thirty thousand acres of tea bushes next appears, the railway running parallel to the road on the opposite side of the valley and the Mahawelli-ganga flowing between. At the

"RIGHT AWAY TO THE FAMOUS KELANI VALLEY."

entrance of Dickoya is Hatton Station, the great centre of the tea districts. A few years ago the site of this important railway station was a marsh, providing good sport in the way of snipe shooting, but now graced by a comfortable hotel, "The Adam s Peak," after the famous sacred mountain visible from its grounds; churches, both English and Roman Catholic; residential bungalows; foundry and workshops; a busy native market; law-courts and police-barracks—all growing up as the outcome of railway extension. Dickoya can boast, too, of one of the best and most appreciated climates of Ceylon. Its elevation of four thousand feet above the sea is sufficient to ensure nights delightfully cool and free from frosts, while the noonday heat is never excessive.

This railway journey into the tea districts is worth making for its own sake, but even the excitement

WAITING FOR THE TRAIN.

of an occasional suspension 'twixt earth and sky over a steep ravine, the wonderful dissolving views of mountain, forest, and stream, and the rapid changes of climate, do not exhaust all the points of interest on this remarkable line. The European traveller will notice with curious interest the gangs of coolies—men, women, and children—some arriving from Southern India, each carrying the sum of his worldly goods, some departing from the coast to return to their native land, others merely leaving one district for another, but all enjoying the freedom of unrestrained conversation in their very limited vocabulary, the subject of wages and food providing the chief topics, and those of paramount concern- Other gangs are noticed engaged in their daily task of plucking or pruning the hardy little tea bushes on the various estates. Nor should we pass over the pretty feature of the numerous bungalows, each

A RUSH FOR SEATS.

situated upon some charming knoll and surrounded by a veritable little paradise. The neat tea factories, too, dotted here and there in the landscape cannot but be noticed, and give the clue to the *raison d'être* of the railway.

We have already remarked that Hatton is a great centre of tea districts. For this reason we shall alight here and make an excursion, as we did at Gampola. There is not much question as to the direction in which we should proceed, for there looms in the distance (twelve miles as the crow flies) that wondrous mountain which has allured to its heights millions of the human race—Adam's Peak; while between us and that venerated spot lies a picturesque stretch of country almost entirely under cultivation of that product in which we are so greatly interested. For about fourteen miles we proceed through a portion of Dickoya, and onwards

KINTYRE MASKELIYA.

through the gap of Maskeliya, where the lovely waterfalls of the Peak burst into view.

Maskeliya is the nearest tea district to the famous mountain. Its extent is about twenty-three thousand acres. The estate which we have chosen for illustration is known as Kintyre. It is situated in the very heart of the district upon the banks of the Maskeliya river, which is one of the feeders of the great Kelaniya-ganga. Like many other tea estates in Ceylon Kintyre was originally a coffee plantation, and one of the first in the Maskeliya district to be adapted for tea on a large scale. In the first instance the tea was planted under the coffee trees when they began to show signs of succumbing to the leaf disease that ultimately ruined the industry. As the tea bushes grew up the coffee was gradually uprooted, giving place to an unbroken expanse of tea, as seen in our photograph.

As we shall shortly inspect the latest methods of tea manufacture, it will be interesting now to inquire in what manner beginnings were made when tea began to oust coffee from these fields. For some time the manufacture was carried on in the corner of the old coffee store. The rolling of the leaf was done by hand, while the firing was accomplished by means of a pit filled with charcoal, over which the trays of rolled leaf were placed. As the little bushes grew to perfection, this primitive and tentative arrangement was succeeded by a large factory fitted with the latest invented machinery driven by steam- and water-power, such as we shall presently describe in all detail.

The success which attended every effort in changing the surface of the coffee land to that of tea must have been an immense relief to the enterprising proprietors, who were facing ruin with desperate courage. Nothing but the most plucky and determined resourcefulness, characteristic of the true Briton, prevented the whole planting community in the early 'eighties from abandoning their estates in despair. But they remained, and it is due to them that Ceylon is still the first and most flourishing of the crown colonies. This fact alone would warrant considerable prominence being given to the tea industry in any description of Ceylon; but too much Tea may be regarded as monotonous, and we will therefore avail ourselves of some diversion wherever opportunity offers. Here, with Adam's Peak towering above us, is a chance not to be lost.

A GROUP OF CANGANIES AT HATTON.

CHAPTER X.

ADAM'S PEAK.

THERE is no object more familiar to the inhabitants of Ceylon, or makes a deeper impression upon the multitudes who visit her shores, than the lofty cone which bears the name of our first parent; and it may be said without fear of contradiction that among all the mountains in the world invested by tradition with superstitious veneration none has stirred the emotions of so many of our fellow-subjects as Adam's Peak. The origin of its sacred character, involved at once as it is in the legendary history of several ancient religions, has been the subject of considerable research and greater conjecture.

There is no doubt that the legends take their rise in the mark on the summit resembling the impress of a gigantic human foot. This the Buddhists devoutly worship as the sacred footprint of Gautama, while the Hindoos equally claim it as that of Siva, and the Mahommedans, borrowing their history from the Jews, as that of Adam. Thus do the adherents of three great religions, to the number of 800,000,000 of our fellow-creatures, vie with one another in veneration of the lonely Peak. As in pilgrim bands they ascend the mighty cone their hearts are moved and they regard its rugged paths as steps unto Heaven. From all parts of Asia thousands annually flock up the steep and rocky track, enduring privation and hardship for the good of their souls. Some of the very old people of both sexes are borne aloft upon the shoulders of their stalwart sons, others struggle upwards unaided, until, fainting by the way, they are considerately carried with all haste in their swooning condition to the summit and forced into an attitude of worship at the shrine to secure the full benefits of their pilgrimage before death should supervene; others never reach the top at all, but perish from cold and fatigue; and there have been many instances of pilgrims losing their lives by being blown over precipices or falling from giddiness induced by a thoughtless retrospect when surmounting especially dangerous cliffs. Some idea of the appalling difficulties that present themselves to those who ascend from the western side may be gathered by a glance at the precipitous shoulder of the rock observable on the right-hand side of our photograph on page 128. The passage of this involves such imminent risk that a false step at any moment would result in a fall of several hundred feet.

The European traveller, although uninfluenced by any superstition, is nevertheless affected by the awe-inspiring prospect that meets his gaze when he has reached the summit. There are many mountains of greater height from whose lofty peaks the eye can scan vast stretches of eternal snow, but none can unfold a scene where Nature asserts herself with such impressive effect as here.

Before describing the chief features of the summit

and the curious shadow phenomenon, some details of the ascent may be of interest. The journey may be accomplished from the south-western or the north-eastern side of the cone, the former being extremely steep and difficult, while the latter is comparatively easy. Pilgrims generally choose the more arduous route, owing to the importance that is attached to the religious rites to be observed at various stages, marked by some cliff or spring to which legends have attributed a sacred character.

A start is made from Ratnapura, the City of Gems, in whose vicinity are found most of the sapphires and cats-eyes of Ceylon. The heat of this place is great when the sun is abroad, and renders the walk through several miles of jungle land very trying, but the path lies through such lovely vegetation that the orchids, pitcher-plants, and other equally beautiful flowers, turn one's mind from the discomforts of the way, which to the European traveller, more heavily handicapped than the native by clothing, are nevertheless very real. After about eight miles we begin to reach a cooler atmosphere, and the scene changes to a landscape of ravines and crags hung with giant creepers in festoons spread from tree to tree and rock to rock. Then we begin to toil up the remaining ten miles of the rocky pilgrimage over gnarled and interlaced roots and relentless obstacles innumerable, at one moment on the edge of a steep abyss, at another traversing narrow passes o'erhung with the boughs of forest trees. At length we reach Ouda Pawanella, a hamlet at the foot of a huge beetling cliff. As we climb on we pass near the edge of a dizzy precipice about eight hundred feet in depth, called Nilihela, after a maiden who incautiously fell over it and was dashed to pieces on the rocks below. Her spirit still haunts the spot, and her voice is heard in the echo that answers to ours. Every open eminence for the rest of the way discloses a prospect both enchanting and magnificent. A toilsome mile farther brings us to Diyabetma, where the Peak now comes into view, and the reverential salutation of the pilgrims, "Saädu!" "Saädu!" breaks the stillness of the dense forest as the goal of their aspirations is revealed to their sight.

Here is a dilapidated bungalow which is now useless to the traveller, being choked up with a rank growth of vegetation. Probably one of the last Europeans who made use of it was Mr. Knighton, who described it as a damp, uncomfortable cell, where all attempt to sleep was vain owing to the roar of elephants and the scream of leopards and monkeys, which alone were sufficient to make night hideous, to say nothing of the possibility of a visit from such unwelcome guests.

Next we come to a romantic bathing-pool, where the Sitaganga, a sacred mountain stream, the subject of a great deal of legendary superstition, provides the pilgrims with holy water for the obligatory purification before they attempt to ascend the precipitous rocks which for the rest of the way now demand the utmost intrepidity.

The most appalling obstacle is reached when the traveller, having climbed to the summit of a precipice, is met by a cliff whose crest literally overhangs the spot upon which he stands. To scale this wall of rock with its projecting cornice without artificial aids would be utterly impossible. An iron ladder, however, has been affixed to the perpendicular wall, and at the top the defiant projection has to be overcome by means of links let into the rock and by the aid of chains attached to the sloping slabs of granite which crown the cliff. The stoutest heart cannot but experience moments of anxiety as this point is reached, and the feet leave the firm ladder to be inserted in the rusty, ill-shaped links. There is nothing between us and the yawning abyss save the links which grate and sway as, with every nerve o'erstrained, we haul ourselves over the next thirty yards of bare and sloping rock. So great is the peril, that the slightest hesitation or the merest glance to right or left might unsteady the nerves and end in a fatal catastrophe.

The history of these rusty chains, with their shapeless links of varying size bearing the unmistakable impress of antiquity, is involved in myth and mystery. The chain near the top is said to have been made by Adam himself, who is believed by all true followers of the Prophet to have been hurled from the seventh heaven of Paradise upon this Peak, where he remained standing on one foot until years of penitence and suffering had expiated his offence. His partner Eve is believed to have fallen near Mecca, and after being separated from her husband for two hundred years, Adam, with the assistance of the angel Gabriel, fetched her to Ceylon as being in his opinion the best substitute for Paradise.

Ashreef, a Persian poet, tells us that we owe the fixing of the chains to Alexander the Great, who "voyaged to Ceylon about B.C. 330, and there devised means whereby he and his friends might ascend the mountain of Serendib, fixing thereto chains with rings and nails and rivets made of iron and brass, so that travellers, by their assistance, may be enabled to climb the mountain, and obtain glory by finding the sepulchre of Adam, on whom be the blessing of Allah!"

Whatever value may be set upon these statements as to the origin of the chains, it is certain that they existed at a very early period. Marco Polo, who visited Ceylon in the thirteenth century, thus refers to them: "In this island there is a very high mountain, so rocky and precipitous that the ascent to the top is impracticable except by the assistance of iron chains employed for that purpose." How they were affixed is a mystery impossible of solution, and I certainly have no theory to advance.

The summit is reached by climbing an almost perpendicular precipice by the aid of a chain called the "chain of the creed," on each link of which the weary pilgrims utter some expression of devotion as they attain to the miniature plateau where their longing hearts are satisfied before the Sri-pada or sacred footprint.

The ascent to the Peak from the north-eastern side is, as we have said, easier than the one described above, and, although it is generally considered less meritorious from the pilgrim's point of view, many forego the benefits to be derived from the more arduous climb in the belief that the additional peril, though by no means supererogatory, is not essential to their sacred duty.

The European traveller is of course quite free in his choice. If he does not care to take his life in his hands up the south-western route, he may journey from Hatton, as we have done, into the Maskeliya district and ascend on this side.

We advance through the forest to Oosamalle, the final ascent to which is made by means of steps cut in the precipitous rocks. This is the last place where water is procurable before the summit is reached. On either side of the ledge will be noticed rude huts, where pilgrims are wont to refresh themselves prior to the task that now awaits them. The beautiful flowering nelu is seen in the

OOSAMALLE.

foreground, and the aged rhododendrons spread their haggard branches above the dilapidated roofing of the hovels.

It is the custom of the Tamils upon making a pilgrimage to provide themselves with supplies of cotton, which they attach to the trees at Oosamalle. Some of these threads may be distinctly seen in our picture hanging from the topmost boughs of the rhododendrons, to which they have been fastened at considerable hazard of life and limb. This curious practice is due to a common belief in the following story: In the days when the Tamils were the masters of Ceylon, their king made a pilgrimage to the Peak, and on his way he shot a deer, wounding it in the leg. Its blood was traced as far as Oosamalle, where the king saw the figure of a man sewing up a wound in his leg. He thereupon exclaimed, "What is this that I have done? I have shot a swamy instead of a deer." He then gave orders that all pilgrims going up the Peak should leave some cotton on the Oosamalle for the swamy, in case he should be shot again and need more thread to sew up his wounds. The Singhalese, however, justify the custom on a different ground, saying that Buddha halted at this spot to sew up a rent in his robe, and they have a curious belief that by fastening threads to any place which has been specially sanctified by Sakya-muni and holding the ends the sacred influence is thereby transmitted, and they receive benefits and favours and even cures for sickness.

It will be noticed that Oosamalle lies at the very foot of the actual cone, and here the ascent in real earnest begins. It is about three miles to the summit, and as the difficulties of the climb on this side may to some extent be realised from an examination of the picture, I shall spare the reader any further description, only adding that similar chains of mysterious origin are found suspended over every cliff presenting great danger, for the assistance of the pilgrims by this route also.

The last glimmer of light was passing away as I clambered into the open space, enclosed within a wall of rock, within which lies the sacred footprint beneath a picturesque little canopy. I had the good fortune to make the ascent in the genial company of a gentleman whose estate lies at the foot of the mountain, and without whose valuable acquaintance with the vernacular, which he placed at my service, my camera at least would never have reached the top. Our retinue of coolies, amongst whom were distributed the necessary provisions and camping paraphernalia for the night, became almost mutinous, complaining bitterly of their burden, and asserting the impossibility of proceeding up the difficult steeps encumbered with its weight. The sorest grievance was the forty pounds of my camera box, which we were determined should not fall behind, for the sole object of the journey was to photograph the remarkable shadow of the Peak as seen in our picture. At length, however, all reached the top in safety, and we immediately set to work with such preparations for the comfort of the inner and outer man as are possible where there is literally no protection from the wind that bites the cheek and chills the bones. How the poor and thinly clad coolies bear the exposure I cannot understand, for with the thickest winter clothing and wrapped in woollen rugs, the cold seemed to us intense. Fires were soon kindled, and the cook who accompanied us served with marvellous alacrity a dinner that would have done credit to a well-appointed kitchen.

The first hours of night were passed in the pleasant talk which is always a natural outcome of excellent toddy accompanied by the fragrant weed. At length Nature's sweet restorer came, and, covered in our wraps, we slept till the buzz of voices told of the approach of dawn. Then came the moments

THE SHADOW OF ADAM'S PEAK

of suspense. Would the atmospheric conditions, without which the shadow is impossible, present themselves? The first faint beams revealed the fleecy shroud of mist covering the world below, and, as clearer grew the welling light, up rose the mighty shadow. Like a distant pyramid it stood for many seconds; then nearer and nearer, ever increasing in size and distinctness as the rays of light broadened over the horizon, it advanced towards us like a veil, through which the distant mountain forests and plains were distinctly visible, till at length it seemed to merge in its mighty parent, and instantly vanished.*

It has been stated that as the shadow approaches the mountain its size diminishes; but this is the opposite of what I saw and the camera recorded. Accounts of this phenomenon are, however, so varying, that doubtless its characteristics differ with the changes of temperature, the density of the vapours, and the direction of the air-currents.

As the shadow departed the mists began to float upwards, revealing a landscape which, by all who have seen it, is unanimously admitted to be amongst the grandest in the world. "No other mountain," wrote Sir Emerson Tennent, "presents the same unobstructed view over land and sea. Around it

* Many photograpers, both professional and amateur, have expressed the opinion that my picture of the Shadow of Adam's Peak, as published in my larger work entitled "Nuwara Eliya and Adam's Peak," is not a genuine photograph. I can only reply that it was printed from the original negative, which exhibits the shadow clearly and well defined and has in no degree been retouched. There is no more or less in the picture than was obtained direct from the negative. The illustration given here is, however, of a different character, being the result of photography and brush combined: the effect is quite true to nature and the particulars are exactly as recorded by my camera.

to the north and east the traveller looks down on the zone of lofty hills that encircle the Kandyan kingdom, whilst to the westward the eye is carried far over undulated plains, threaded by rivers like cords of silver, till in the purple distance the glitter of the sunbeams on the sea marks the line of the Indian Ocean."

CHAPTER XI.

DIMBULA.

WE now return to Hatton and make our way one more stage by rail to Talawakelle, in the great Dimbula district, where we shall vary the monotony of passing through tea estates by an examination of the various processes by which the leaves are converted into the manufactured article. As we move slowly

S. CLAIR ESTATE. (SEE ALSO PAGE 46.)

upwards the atmosphere is so crisp and refreshing that it is difficult to realise that we are in the latitude of Colombo and within six degrees of the equator. After passing Kotagala, the loveliness of the scenery increases until it seems to reach its climax as the remarkable beauty of St. Clair Falls unfolds itself just before we reach Talawakelle. We see the Kotmale River flowing through the valley several hundred feet below, while in the distance towers aloft the grand range known as the "Great Western," whose highest point is some seven thousand feet above the sea.

Dimbula is the largest of all the tea districts, and contains estates to the aggregate extent of fifty

THE GREAT WESTERN, DIMBULA

thousand acres. It is well served with means of communication; the railway runs right through it, winding about its mountain sides for twenty miles, and reaching the elevation of five thousand feet; while splendid roads penetrate its various divisions. One of these, known as the Agra Patnas, is second to none for its complete combination of all the characteristics of climate and soil that have been found suitable for the production of the highest class of Ceylon Tea. It has what is known as a perfect tea-climate; and the formation of the hills ensures freedom from damage by wind, which in many districts is a danger that has to be combated by the growth of extensive belts of grevilleas and gums for shelter. I do not say that none are necessary in the Agras, but fewer than in more exposed country. The climate of Dimbula, especially in

LOGIE ESTATE, LINDULA.

the Lindula and Agra Patnas divisions, is as near perfection as need be desired. Its average shade temperature is about 65° Fahr., and it may be said that the variation is from 55° to 70°. The rainfall is about one hundred inches for the year, and is fairly distributed. After warning, by the gradual increase in the density of the vapours, it descends in true tropical fashion, with long intervals of sunshine between the storms.

To visit the Agras we leave the railway at Talawakelle, where a good road passes through the fine subdivision of Lindula for about five miles, and thence for twelve miles through the Agra district, at the end of which we reach Diyagama, the utmost estate and one of the finest in Ceylon.

First of all Talawakelle Bazaar will arrest attention; for it is one of the liveliest of native trading quarters. Here the labourers, men, women, and children, of a hundred estates are supplied with

RESTING PLACE FOR TRANSPORT CATTLE.

their luxuries, which consist chiefly of trinkets, sweets, curry stuffs, and cloths of many colours which, without any tailoring, serve them as wearing apparel. Here, too, the native rice-contractors have their stores, which are of no small importance in a country where the soil is cultivated only for the production of an export luxury, and the food of the labourer is an imported article. We notice also in this busy native town long rows of sheds and stations for the hundreds of humped bulls that do the work of transport for the whole of the Lindula and Agra districts. Loads of tea are always to be seen in course of transit to the railway, drawn by pairs of these fine beasts of burden. The subject whose special portrait is here given is a good specimen of the Mysore breed, enjoying his bath by the wayside. The curious brands upon his skin, which seem to be the result of unnecessary cruelty, are probably in-

A GOOD SPECIMEN OF THE MYSORE BREED.

tended to have a decorative effect, but in some cases such treatment is begun as a remedy for lameness or rheumatism, and afterwards continued for ornament. The Tamil characters on his shoulder, Navena Rena (*Anglice N. R.*), are the initials of the owner. A pair of such animals would draw more than a ton of tea up the steep incline by the mere pressure of their humps against a huge cross-bar resting upon their necks and attached in the centre to the pole of the cart. In the days of coffee planting, before the railway was made, such a pair would take down to the port of Colombo a hundred and twenty bushels of coffee, with the necessary food for the journey, at the rate of twenty miles a day.

But we are somewhat digressing, and we will return for a few moments to the bazaar, where we notice that the stalls are all open to view, even as they are at the lower and warmer elevations; the

TALAWAKELLE BAZAAR.

natives, however, clothe their backs in these cooler regions, although their legs are generally bare. The necessity for clothing creates a market for the *cumbly*, a rug of coarse sacking, which in wet weather both men and women fold in a curious manner so that it will hang suspended from the head and fall over the shoulders and back; but many are the comical sights of Tamils attired in cast-off coats of livery or military tunics, with their legs bare beneath the tails. Some years ago there was a trade done between Europe and this country in soiled and disused military tunics, which were imported by the thousand and disposed of to coolies at a couple of rupees; but the practice is now disallowed. These garments, however, do duty for the coolie for many long years, and numbers are still to be seen. But for the present we are bent upon seeing the growth

THE AGRA OYA FLOWING BETWEEN BEARWELL AND BELGRAVIA ESTATES.

and manufacture of tea, and we will therefore leave our further consideration of the labourer who tends these operations till afterwards.

The longest feeder of the Mahawelliganga (the great sandy river), whose acquaintance we made at Peradeniya, is the Agra Oya, which takes its rise at Kirigalpotta, a mountain reaching an altitude of 7,732 feet, near the Horton plains. This river flows through the Agra district, and as we wend our way around the hillsides it is always present, meandering in the valleys beneath us and in close approximation. In flood it is a roaring torrent, but after the rains have subsided it becomes a picturesque and shallow river flowing amongst the thousands of massive granite boulders that have during long ages of time become detached from the mountains and rolled into its bed.

Our little pictures give glimpses of this river and the tea estates which lie upon its banks. Here we see a factory on some spot where the utility of the stream has given it a place-value by the saving of steam power; there we notice a bungalow upon some site chosen for its beautiful aspect; and as we drive along the well-made metalled road we notice that every acre, with the exception of some patanas, or grass lands, from which the district derives its name, is well covered with tea plants, looking unmistakably healthy, and suggesting at once the perfect "tea climate" to which we have made reference.

At about the twelfth mile we arrive at an estate which is peculiarly suitable for our purpose of examining in detail the cultivation and manufacture of tea: it is Sutton, the property of Mr. J. Stewart, who courteously welcomes us and offers every facility at his command both in field and factory. The estate is very precipitous, as will at once be seen upon reference to our view, which contains the bungalow. It has its flats, like most estates in these mountain districts, but it rises above them somewhat abruptly for one thousand feet, and at the top reaches an elevation above sea level of 5,300 feet. If we glance for a moment at our picture of the principal

SUTTON ESTATE IN THE AGRA PATNAS.

steep on this page we shall see that the hardy tea plant grows vigorously almost out of the very rock itself, and this suggests to us at once how very much depends upon climate as well as soil for the production of those splendid qualities in the manufactured article, which make Ceylon tea the finest in the world. The soil upon these rocky eminences, although to a great extent supplied by the forests that

THE HARDY TEA PLANT GROWING ALMOST OUT OF THE VERY ROCK ITSELF.

once clothed them, must originally have been formed by the action of the climate itself. Such is the nature of this climate, that the most solid rock is forced to decompose in sufficient degree to nourish some of the most beautiful forms of vegetable life. That great endowment of the human race—the soil—is actually produced upon these rocky mountains by the hand of Nature herself. An absolutely bare rock is seldom found. The abundant rainfall and the heat combined seem to pulverise the hardest surface, and to bring out latent forces from which springs food for man and beast.

Exhaustion of the soil was a doctrine much preached in connection with the great coffee failures, and there is no doubt as to the truth contained in it. Fertility has often been destroyed outright by the wanton abuse of Nature; and even in this fertile land, where the climatic elements are so favourable to production, the enterprising European planter frequently miscalculates the amount which Nature is prepared to bestow. There remains, however, the fact that even the undecomposed rocks constitute a wonderful store, from which human wants are being supplied by process of nature, though slowly and in small degree. It is only the already decomposed surface that is subject to immediate exhaustion; there still remains a fund for future supplies, and upon such a natural endowment the human race has lived for ages past. Whether Nature's funds are now being too severely drawn upon is a question which may materially affect the future, but the present generation of planters, judging from the healthy appearance of the fields, would seem to have little to fear.

We will now take in due order the daily round of the planter's life. To him the adage "early to bed and early to rise" is something more than a mere opinion. He rises at early dawn, which in this country varies only some minutes throughout the year, and at 6 a.m. attends the muster of all the coolies employed on the estate. These comprise men, women, and children of about eleven years and upwards, who assemble in gangs near the factory or other convenient spot. Each gang

THE CANGANY OR TASKMASTER

is in charge of a cangany or taskmaster, who superintends the work of the labourers, chastises them for their shortcomings, and (on his own account) looks after their finances, not always disinterestedly. The cangany plays an important part not only in the management of, but in supplying the labourers, and we shall have more to say about him later. The conductor, too, is another official who puts in an appearance and holds an even more important position. He is the superintendent's right-hand man in the fields; he understands the art of cultivation and looks after the various gangs. The tea-maker who superintends the work inside the factory is also there; for work in every department begins with the break of day. All appear as if by magic at the blast of a horn or the sound of a tom-tom. The superintendent arrives on the scene, counts them, and assigns them in gangs to various work; some to plucking, others to pruning, weeding, and clearing surface drains. He then recounts them and enters the number assigned to each work, in order that he may be able to check them at the end of the day. Early tea, that simple term used in Ceylon to denote the Indian *chota hazari* or little breakfast, is the next item in the superintendent's programme, and he returns to his bungalow for this repast. The factory is next visited; and everything there being found satisfactory he proceeds to the fields and inspects the work of the pluckers. Here he walks carefully along the lines of women and children who are plucking the young grown leaves.

In our picture may be seen some pluckers at work. The baskets, which they carry suspended by ropes from their heads and into which they cast the leaves over their shoulders, hold about fourteen pounds weight when full. At the end of each row of trees is placed a large transport basket, into which the leaves are emptied from time to time as the baskets become full. Women are preferred to men for this work, and earn as much as twenty-five cents, or about fourpence a day. They are not always the wives of the male coolies of the estate; many of them come over from India to seek the high rate of wages above mentioned. They look very picturesque, with their fine glossy hair and dreamy black eyes, their ears, necks, arms, and ankles adorned with silver ornaments, and their gay cloths of many colours falling in graceful folds while standing intent upon their work among the bushes. To such an extent does practice accelerate the action of eye, brain, and the march of their nimble fingers, that it is difficult for the uninitiated to believe how carefully chosen is each leaf or shoot. Plucking is a most important branch of the tea planter's business, and requires careful teaching and constant supervision. Only the young and succulent leaves can be used in the manufacture, and the younger the leaf the finer the quality of the tea; so that if a specially delicate quality is desired, only the bud and two extreme leaves of each shoot will be taken; whereas if a large yield is wanted, as many as four leaves may be plucked from the top of the shoot downwards, but with the result of a proportionately poorer quality of the manufactured article. There are many other points in the art of tea plucking that require care and judgment, as, for instance, the eye or bud in the axil of the leaf plucked must be left uninjured on the branch; and in case of special grades of tea

A TRIO OF PLUCKERS.

THE UNMERCIFUL TREATMENT OF DISMEMBERMENT.

being required the selection of particular leaves is of the utmost importance.

Although a tea estate has no hedgerows or distantly visible boundaries it is nevertheless divided into fields for convenience of treatment, and each field is visited in turn by the superintendent. Weeding is very effectively and thoroughly carried out. It would astonish farmers in the old country to hear that in Ceylon the tea fields are weeded on contract at the rate of about one shilling and fourpence for each acre per month, and that upon this system they are kept almost entirely free from weeds and grass. Indeed, it may be said that the tea gardens of Ceylon are kept far cleaner than most of the flower gardens of England.

If left to Nature the tea plant will grow to the height of about twenty feet, with a circumference of about the same; but the artifice of the planter keeps it down to about three feet by constant prunings. After a year or two of plucking the plant naturally loses vitality to send forth abundance of new shoots; it then receives the unmerciful treatment of dismemberment; its branches are lopped off to such an extent that it looks utterly ruined. But as though its vital parts had appreciated the rest it bursts forth with renewed vigour, and in a very few weeks is prepared for the ordeal of another year's constant plucking. It is the practice in some cases to prune somewhat lightly every year and in others to treat the plants with heavier pruning biennially.

But we are anticipating, and it will perhaps be better to explain the treatment of the plant in its earliest stages of growth. It is planted in the fields either as seed or in the form of young plants taken

THEIR DWELLINGS WHICH ARE CALLED "LINES" (*page* 159).

from a nursery. Each plant is allotted twelve square feet of surface soil, and thus we may say that a fully planted up acre contains 3,630 plants. An important consideration in planting out the young seedlings which are raised in the nursery is the "lining" or placing them so that each may obtain the fullest exposure to the sun, in order that when they reach maturity the plucking service, which wholly depends upon the sun's influence, may be as great as possible. Opinions differ as to the age at which plucking may begin, but it depends greatly upon the elevation of the estate above sea level, the growth being naturally less rapid in the cooler altitudes. We may, however, say roughly that in the low country, from sea level to two thousand feet, tea plants will mature for plucking in two years, and upon the higher elevations in four years. But about a year before the plant thus comes into bearing for purposes of tea manufacture it is cut down to about nine inches or a foot from the ground; and again the same operation is performed two inches higher than the first cutting a couple of months before plucking begins. The plant is now plucked regularly every eight or nine days for two years, when it is again cut down to a couple of inches above the last cut. It will be seen from the foregoing remarks that in the matter of pruning the younger bushes are treated somewhat differently from the older ones, inasmuch as the young ones are allowed to retain a larger proportion of their recent growth.

The novice who tries his hand with the pruning knife will be surprised at the hard labour of the task and the discomfort of the stooping attitude that must be adopted; and when it is considered that a field of about fifty acres contains some two hundred thousand bushes the amount of toil involved will become apparent. Of course male coolies only are employed at this work, and they become so remarkably dexterous that what seems to the novice a task of great exertion becomes to them one of comparative ease.

The branches which are lopped off in the process of pruning are for the most part left where they fall; but as many fall into and obstruct the surface drains it is necessary to put on coolies to clear them out. A space of about six feet on either side of the drain is thus kept entirely clear, so that there may be no impediment to the flow of the surface water. It is, however, considered advisable, in seasons of much blight, to bury or burn the prunings, and this method has recently been very extensively adopted.

It is now about ten o'clock and the baskets of the most dexterous pluckers should be nearly full. The superintendent therefore returns to them and notes against their names the weight of leaf plucked by each, after which the baskets are emptied and the leaf conveyed to the factory. This operation is repeated two or three times in the course of the day. At four o'clock the pluckers cease work and carry off their baskets to the factory, where they sort over the leaf upon mats spread on the ground, as shown in our picture, and cast out any very coarse leaf that may have been accidentally plucked. The number of pounds plucked by each coolie is again entered in the check roll against his or her name, and then the sum of each plucker's efforts passes before the eye of the superintendent before the coolies are dismissed; and woe betide him, or her,

SORTING THE LEAF AT DEWY EVE.

"THE SUM OF EACH PLUCKER'S EFFORTS PASSES BEFORE THE EYE OF THE SUPERINTENDENT."

who has not a goodly weight accounted for. Laziness thus detected brings a fine of half pay and in many cases a taste of the cangany's stick.

But we were describing the daily round of the superintendent, and at present we have not pursued it beyond the early morning visits to various works in the field. Some four hours spent in this occupation in the pure mountain air, upon the rocky steeps that we have described, produces a fairly healthy appetite for food and drink, and the next consideration is therefore the inner man. The planter returns to his bungalow for breakfast at about eleven, and generally spends the afternoon in attention to correspondence. At four the sound of the tom-tom, horn, or whistle, according to the custom of the estate, summons the coolies from the fields to the muster ground, where the superintendent now marks them down in the check-roll for their day's pay. In case of bad or insufficient work the offender is marked down as "sick," which means no pay at all for that day; or he gets what is termed "half a name," which means half pay. Now they depart to their dwellings, which are called "lines." A coolie line is usually a long building of one storey only, divided into a large number of compartments. Each compartment accommodates about four coolies, and it is obvious that they do not enjoy the luxury of much space; but their ideas of comfort are not ours, and they are better pleased to lie huddled together upon the mud floors of these tiny hovels than to occupy superior apartments. Their condition calls for no pity or sympathy, as we shall see later; for in many respects they are a favoured class.

We have now dealt with a day's field-work: we have seen how the raw material is obtained; but we have still to examine the various processes by which it is converted into the manufactured article. For this purpose we visit the factory. Here the green leaf undergoes four distinct processes, known as withering, rolling, fermenting, and firing. We will take these in due order; and first as to withering:

Let us deal with the green leaf that has been plucked on Monday and brought to the factory as before described. It is received by the tea maker, who ascertains its net weight, which he enters in a book. It is then passed on to an upper storey, where it is spread thinly on shelves of jute hessian and left to wither. Our illustration of this process will give a better idea of the shelves and the method of spreading the leaves than many words of description. These shelves are sometimes made of wire instead of jute, but jute hessian very loosely woven so that the air can pass freely through it is mostly used for this purpose. Successful withering depends very much on good light, warm temperature, and a dry atmosphere. The last named is often the most difficult to obtain, and upon wet dull days it has to be produced by artificial means. In fair weather the leaf will wither naturally in about eighteen or twenty hours, but as the weather varies and climates vary in different districts there can be no time rule to guide the tea maker. When it is explained that the object of withering the leaf is to allow the sap and other moisture to evaporate until the leaf assumes a particular degree of softness and flaccidity, which renders it susceptible to a good twist by the roller in the next process, it will be realised how important a thing it is for the tea maker to judge of the exact moment when these conditions have been reached and the withering must terminate.

WITHERING THE LEAF.

ROLLING THE LEAF.

The leaf, being withered to this exact extent, is swept together and conveyed to the lower floor by means of a shoot. Here it is put into a machine called a roller. The object of rolling is to squeeze out the tannin and any moisture left over after the withering and to give the leaf a good twist. It is difficult to describe a tea roller, or to illustrate its effective parts by a photograph of the complete machine in working; our illustration should, however, assist us to understand it sufficiently with the following explanation: The lower part may be regarded as a table with cylindrical ribs attached to its surface and a trap door in the centre. Suspended above this table is a smaller surface opposed to it, and the two surfaces are moved in opposite directions by a crank with an eccentric motion. The upper surface is open in the centre, and extending upwards from the opening is a funnel or box to receive the withered leaf, which being therein placed the two surfaces are set in motion by steam or other power, and the leaf is thus rolled and twisted between the two surfaces. The lid of the funnel or box is gradually screwed down as rolling proceeds and in this way the pressure upon the leaf is regulated. The appearance of the leaf or "roll," as it is technically termed, when taken out of the roller is a mess of mashy lumps.

It is next put through a roll-breaker, which not only breaks up the balls or lumps into which the leaves have formed but sifts the small and fine leaf through a wire mesh on to a cloth placed below to receive it. The roll-breaker, which may be seen in our illustration on page 165, operates on the leaf by means of rapidly revolving shafts to which are attached iron forks that beat against the balls as they are cast into the funnel.

It is by the use of rolling machinery that Ceylon tea is kept pure and free from the dirt which finds its way into the teas of China, where the operation is performed by the hands of the bland but unwashed Ah Sin.

The leaf is next spread out in wooden frames, and having been covered by wet cloths is allowed to ferment until it attains a bright copper tint such as the infused leaves have in the tea-pot; or at least should have, for the brighter they appear the better the tea. The rolling process, by breaking the cells of the leaf, induces fermentation, which is a very necessary stage of the manufacture, the character of the tea when made depending greatly on the degree to which fermentation is allowed to continue. When the commodity known as green tea is required, the fermentation is checked at once so that no change of colour may take place; but to produce black tea the process must be carried on for a considerable time, the sufficiency of which is determined by the smell and appearance of the leaf—points that require considerable experience and care, since over-fermentation completely spoils the quality.*

Fermentation being complete, the tea is now transferred to the apparatus known as the desiccator, where it undergoes the process known as firing. There are numerous kinds of desiccators, the one here illustrated being that used in Sutton factory. The fermented leaf is spread thinly upon wire trays,

* In the Kelani Valley and other districts of the low country where the climate is much hotter very little fermenting is necessary. The leaves are spread out thinly for a short time and firing may then be proceeded with.

ROLLER AND ROLL-BREAKER.

THE DESICCATOR.

which are pushed one after the other into this machine, where a current of hot air from 210° to 220° Fahr. is made to pass through them. The tea emerges from the desiccator perfectly dry and brittle, and of a black colour. It is now completely manufactured. The tea maker next weighs it and enters the amount of "made tea" against the leaf which he received on Monday, and it should be found to be lighter by 75 per cent. The actual ratio of green leaf to "made tea" works out at about 4,200 lbs. of green leaf to 1,000 lbs. of manufactured tea.

Monday's plucking, which has now by Tuesday night been converted into tea, is placed into bins, with wire meshed lids, to cool, and on Wednesday morning it goes through the process of sifting, which sorts it up into the various grades known commercially as Broken Orange Pekoe, Orange Pekoe, Pekoe, Souchong, and Dust, all of which terms are of Chinese origin, and refer to some characteristic of the sort of tea they represent.

The sifter is a machine consisting of a series of sieves one above the other in the form of sloping trays with wire meshes. The top tray has a mesh large enough to admit all but the coarsest leaf; the mesh of the second one is somewhat smaller, and the third and fourth decrease in like manner. This sequence of meshes, varying in their apertures, is designed to allow the tea to practically sift itself, inasmuch as each sieve arrests a particular grade, the smallest leaf falling through all the sieves. These sieves or trays are made to oscillate at a very high rate of speed, the power being supplied from the factory engine. It will be seen from our illustration that the sifter automatically ejects the various grades by means of spouts from which it falls into chests.

Everything, it will be observed, is done to avoid handling the tea. Indeed, from the bush to the tea table such methods of pure cleanliness are observed as scarcely any other food manufacture can claim; and especially do these methods of Ceylon tea manufacture stand in contrast to those of China, where the primitive operations employed are such that the stomach would rebel against a detailed description. I am convinced that if the public generally did but realise this difference between Ceylon tea and that of some other countries the demand for the Ceylon article would increase quite beyond the capacity of the country to supply it.

But I am digressing. There is yet something more to be said about the tea as it comes from the sifter. The smallest "leaf" which finds its way to the bottom of the sifter is known as "tea dust." It makes good tea; but the *crême de la crême* of Ceylon tea is that which is arrested by the fourth sieve, known commercially as Broken Orange Pekoe. It is fine and small tea, consisting to a great extent of young tips which look like little chips of wood. These tips not only give the tea a good appearance, but they add greatly to its strength and flavour when infused, as they are the essence of the leaf. Golden Tips alone would be far too strong for the tea-pot, but sometimes they have been separated from the other leaves and sold as pure golden tips. They may be separated by throwing the tea against a big sheet of jute-hessian, to which the tips adhere and the remainder falls to the ground. Small quantities of Ceylon golden tips obtained in this manner have been sold in London for as much as £10

SIFTING THE MANUFACTURED TEA.

to £35 per pound weight. This statement will appear surprising to those who do not already know of the excitement caused by certain auction sales of Ceylon tea about ten years ago. A parcel of this extraordinary tea was first sent from Gartmore Estate in Maskeliya. Its unusual character was quickly recognised by the dealers, and bidding began at £1 1s. per lb., advancing smartly to £10 12s. 6d., at which price it was knocked down. Naturally other planters followed suit with parcels of carefully chosen tips, and £17 was reached by Haviland Estate. Gartmore, however, again came to the front with £25 10s.; but successful attempts were made to reach even a higher price than this, and before the excitement abated the fabulous sum of £35 per lb. was obtained.

The Broken Orange Pekoe travels along the lowest tray till it reaches the end of the machine, where it falls into its box, from which it is removed, weighed again, and transferred to bins reserved for its special grade. The other grades, Orange Pekoe, Pekoe, and Souchong, are all treated in like manner, each falling from the sifter into its special box. The tea maker enters in the factory book the weight of each grade after sifting, and checks it by the aggregate weight entered before sifting.

The percentages of the various grades in relation to the aggregate amount of leaf plucked varies somewhat according to the method of plucking, whether fine or medium. Fine plucking on this estate works out on an average as follows :—

Broken Orange Pekoe	30%	Pekoe Souchong	7%
Orange Pekoe	40%	Dust	3%
Pekoe	19%	Wastage	1%

The different grades are day by day stored away in their separate bins, until there is enough to make what is technically known as a "break," which means a sufficient quantity to place on the market—say 6,000 lbs. and upwards.

The next operation is "bulking," a process simple enough, but of very real importance. The whole contents of the bins of one grade are thrown out and moved by scoops or shovels until it becomes so thoroughly mixed that one pound of tea is quite certain to be equal to another in flavour and appearance. This bulking is necessary to ensure a uniformity of quality throughout a grade of tea which has been plucked and made on different days. The term "factory bulked," when marked upon the chests in which the tea is packed for shipment, indicates that the above operations have taken place, and is a guarantee of uniform quality. It is imperative that the planter should give most careful attention to this matter, as buyers are entitled to reject any break that does not prove to be evenly bulked; and, moreover, teas discovered to be unevenly bulked when they arrive in the London customs are liable to be rebulked at the expense of the grower before removal.

Packing is the next operation. Each chest is lined with lead, and weighed carefully with its little packet of hoop iron and nails necessary for finally securing the lid. The gross weight of each is noted, and filling then commences. This is generally done by machinery. The chest is placed on a platform which oscillates and revolves at about two thousand five hundred revolutions a minute; the tea being poured in is thus shaken so that the utmost

FILLING CHESTS OF TEA FOR SHIPMENT.

A CIRCLE OF SINGHALESE GIRLS FILLING THE LEAD.

THE PACKETING PROCESS IN FULL OPERATION.

capacity of the chest is occupied. All this is done so accurately that the full chest contains its allotted net weight to an ounce. A sheet of lead is now placed on the top and soldered down, thus securing the contents from air or moisture. The lids now being nailed on and the hoop iron attached, the chests are ready for the final operation of marking with the estate name, the grade, and the gross and net weight, after which they are ready for despatch to the tea market. But not all the tea grown and manufactured in Ceylon is thus despatched in chests. There is a growing and important trade done in Ceylon packeted tea, which, it should be noted, carries with it a guarantee of genuineness which no other has. The value of this guarantee cannot be over-estimated, and it consists in the special wrapper of the Ceylon grower or merchant covering the leaden packet. When this wrapper bears a local imprint, as it generally does, the guarantee of a genuine article is still further strengthened. We see this packeting process in full operation in our full-page illustrations. Here the Co-operative Tea Garden Company are packeting their tea. A circle of Singhalese girls, nicely clad and perfectly clean, are at work filling the lead. They take the tea from the heap in the centre and press it into the packet, not with their hands, but with wooden pressure mallets. The packets are then passed on to the boys at the circular table here illustrated, who solder down the lead and in turn pass on the packets to the other girls, who may be seen sitting in rows at the tables and affixing the outer labels. This tea packeting room is no less than four hundred feet in length, and accommodates a thousand workers at one time. It is one of several on the extensive premises of Messrs. Bosanquet & Co., merchants of Colombo and shippers for the company above referred to.

That tea planting is an active and busy life will be gathered from the foregoing sketch of the daily round, and it may not be untrue to say that the planter as a rule works hard. Perhaps it is equally true that he plays harder. In this and many other districts life is by no means all work, nor does it mean, as it used to do in the early coffee days, banishment from the amenities of social life. The Agra district has its sporting, social, and athletic clubs, and a very picturesque ground for cricket, football, and hockey, while the Radella racecourse, which we illustrate on page 195, is within a few miles. We shall consider the facilities which Ceylon offers to the athlete later; but we cannot refrain from giving here an illustration of croquet amongst the tea. The great increase in the popularity of this game has penetrated even the tea estates, and many are the courts to be seen amongst the monotonous little bushes. We restrict our illustrations as much as possible to scenes of everyday life, in order that no disappointment may result to the visitor through impressions first gained from this book. Therefore no "at home" party or special function is taking place here. The court is wet from a heavy shower, and the players are making the best of it. The little picture is, however, suggestive. The presence of ladies and the nature of the game in which they are engaged afford an example of amelioration from the conditions of thirty years ago, when planting in Ceylon was a lonely life.

CROQUET AMONGST THE TEA.

CHAPTER XII.

THE TAMIL COOLIE.

WE have already hinted that the Tamil coolie or labourer on a Ceylon estate is a favoured individual. We shall now consider to what circumstances this is due. When the British capitalist began to explore and cultivate the unkown regions of Ceylon he found no suitable labour supply at hand. The mountain districts were almost uninhabited, and the Singhalese who dwelt in the plains were too well satisfied with their lot to be roused to industry by a new enterprise. But on the adjoining continent were millions of people born to till the soil, whose earnings in their native land amounted only to the miserable pittance of about three farthings a day, while in times of famine, which occurred then, as now, with lamentable frequency, wages vanished altogether. Even at the present day the sum mentioned represents the full earnings of more than half the labourers of southern India. Could not some of these be induced to emigrate to Ceylon? They had but to cross a few miles of sea and walk a hundred miles or so to reach a paradise compared to their own Tinevelly and Madura, where they might increase their earnings ten-fold and return one day to become landowners and capitalists in their own country. From this necessity to import labour arose the system of canganies and "Coast Advances," which is still in vogue to some extent for attracting coolies from the mainland. The method is somewhat as follows: The cangany receives a sum of money from the planter with which

COOLIES' HOMESTEADS IN THE HIGHLANDS.

to engage gangs of coolies in the Indian villages and to pay for their transport. With this he starts on his quest. He details the wonderful story of Ceylon and high wages to the villagers, telling them how easily they can earn and save and return, till he obtains a sufficient number; and then after the few formalities with the Zemindar's man, whom he possibly bribes with the gift of a few rupees or an umbrella to make matters swift and easy, he sets out with his gang for the coast, advances their passage and conducts them to the estate. The system has little changed since the early days. Millions have been brought over, and millions have returned to their villages better and richer in every way for their enterprise.

The Tamil coolie in Ceylon may be a shocking barbarian in point of intellect and civilisation as compared with his British master, but having regard

COOLIES' HOMESTEADS IN THE LOWLANDS.

to his own race and opportunities he is by no means an unfortunate or despicable creature. Compared with his condition at home he is much better off here, where he is free, well housed, his food guaranteed him and medical comforts provided; he is allowed vegetable and fruit gardens, and if he is thrifty he will keep his fowls and goats; he is never oppressed by his master, who generally respects his customs and prejudices. His own ideas, it may be remarked, are few; his vocabulary a very limited one, although he uses it to an inordinate extent; his tastes are very simple, and he usually lives in peace with his neighbour.

In the old coffee days planters were entirely dependent on this immigrant labour. The Singhalese had a great repugnance to work on the estates in the mountain districts except in the initial process of felling forests, and labour supply was consequently a source of anxiety to the pioneer. It is still to be counted an important factor in the economics of the tea industry, although the Singhalese have been attracted to the new culture in no small degree by its suitability to their slender physique, and their increased confidence in the European employer. The extension of planting at the lower and warmer elevations, and the increased means of communication in every direction, have doubtless had their influence also in attracting Singhalese labour. The absence of cart-roads and railways at one time necessitated the transport of produce upon coolies' heads over rugged paths and for great distances. The Tamil will tackle this arduous labour, but the more effeminate Singhalese is not prepared to earn his rice by so much sweat of the brow. Even now in some districts the chests of tea have to be carried by the coolies for some miles; but it is exceptional.

The Singhalese, then, may be said to be taking kindly to the new industry and new conditions, and it is hoped that, as time goes on, Ceylon will be less dependent on immigrant labour. The number of labourers at present employed on the estates may be roughly estimated at one for each acre under cultivation, and the total is approximately

400,oco. If only seven per cent. of these are Singhalese it is a hopeful sign, considering how recently they have been attracted to the occupation. But an important consideration is the number of Tamils now born in the country who grow up here and never leave it. Ramasamy was not always noted for bringing up children, and in the coffee days infant

RAMASAMY'S CHILDREN.

mortality was appalling; but now that children have been found to be well fitted for the work of leaf plucking he finds it useful to preserve his progeny, and little brown urchins of both sexes from the age of five earn their ten to twelve cents a day. Many of them wear very little clothing, as may be noticed in our picture, although the early mornings when they turn out to work at day-break are, in the higher districts, very cold.

These children if not reared upon tea are indeed brought up amongst the bushes. No sooner are they born than they accompany their mothers in the work of plucking. It is an amusing spectacle for the stranger to see them, literally small gangs of suckling humanity basking in the sun upon mother earth, or upon the cumblies of their parents spread out for them upon the estate paths, or amongst the bushes where the work of plucking is going on,

SMALL GANGS OF SUCKLING HUMANITY.

many months before their baby legs have developed sufficiently to support them in any other position. It is no uncommon thing to see half a score of them with one small gang of female pluckers. As they reach the more troublesome age when they begin to feel their feet, the mother does not run the risk of perhaps finding her offspring face downwards in a drain, or descended to the foot of a precipice; she is careful of her progeny in these days for the reason hinted above, and secures the wee bairn by converting the *cumbly* into a temporary hammock, which, with the babe placed within, she suspends from a branch of the nearest tree, visiting the little brown urchin when hunger gives it voice that warns her of the necessity for comfort.

These small details of native life have their bearing on the future prosperity of the industry, however trivial they may seem. Many of these children will

THE STEADY INCREASE OF THE SINGHALESE.

never leave Ceylon, and the future will see a large indigenous Tamil population, which, with the steady increase of the Singhalese, should render the labour supply secure. Moreover, the wealthy Singhalese are themselves entering extensively upon tea cultivation, and this will doubtless have its effect also upon their countrymen of the labouring class.

The thoughts of the Tamil labourer that are not devoted to his food and his pay are, of course, given to Hindu religious belief and superstitions. Their inborn inclination to saami worship, with its weird demon rights of the most ignorant type, holds them in awe of the supernatural, and impels them to attribute their sicknesses and misfortunes to most unnatural causes. Barbarous festivals contribute to their joys; these are more or less connected with the Hindu religion, but are not always strictly in accordance with it; for we notice that what Hinduism contemplates as great sin is frequently prominent in their ceremonies. But if we can realise the extreme ignorance of the coolies, the basest forms of religious worship and the barbarous forms of amusement which they practice will not surprise us. To this picture, however, there is a brighter side gradually gaining ground. European missionary work is being steadfastly carried on with appreciable effect, and it is to be hoped that the rising generation, born to stay in this favoured land, will to a great extent be regenerated, and that Christianity will gain more and more ground amongst them. To satisfactorily civilize and convert the older Tamil coolies would be a Herculean task, and the chief ground of difficulty would be their utter inability to comprehend the true meaning of words used by their teachers. Every idea which the European endeavours to convey to them becomes perverted by their peculiar native mental application of the expressions used. The desired end is therefore advisedly aimed at through the medium of training the young. The Tamil coolie, born and brought up with a miserable conception even of his native creed, has not generally the mental power to grasp anything better, and it is therefore reasonable that a little mental training to the young will give the missionary improved material to deal with. From this point of view estate schools are important. They are very modest institutions, as will be seen from our picture; generally an open thatched shed with perhaps a chair for the school-master, while the pupils sit upon the mud floor; nevertheless they suffice, and are perhaps better than more pretentious arrangements; for it must be borne in mind that a little too much education and unaccus-

SCHOOL ON A TEA ESTATE.

tomed luxury would unfit these children for their calling, or indeed for anything. Freedom they will always enjoy under British rule; but a just and almost paternal control, and a hand almost sparing in the direction of philanthropy are best suited to their needs. Just as the unwise poor laws* of George the Third entirely frustrated the desired amelioration, and tended to pauperise the masses

* Especially the Act known as Gilbert's Act.

in England, so would an injudicious benevolence towards the Tamil coolie render him useless for any purpose. The ill-advised provision for the poor in England above referred to is perhaps not quite analogous, but its effect was the destruction of industrial self-sufficiency. The outcome of treating the Tamil estate labourer in like manner, too considerately, would be laziness and industrial degeneracy. Never does the thoughtful European so much realise the restrictions on his power for good as when dealing with this class of humanity; but his power for evil is unlimited. The coolie now understands that if he would eat he must work, and whatever may be done to improve his condition by means of education or otherwise, this idea must not be eradicated. But there is little likelihood at present that the Tamil coolie will receive a surfeit of philanthropic attention. We have stated that he is a favoured individual considering his original native condition in India. The temporal advantages which he enjoys are the gifts of legislation, and are perhaps fully adequate. It is, however, very difficult for the missions to supply all that is desirable for his moral and spiritual welfare; yet the light is radiating, and it is certain that many of the superintendents of estates are exerting their personal influence for the general good of the labourers in their employ.

We have had glimpses of the life of these Tamil men, women, and children throughout our journeyings from Kandy upwards, and our acquaintance with them will now suffice. The Singhalese labourer will call for further consideration when we reach the lower elevations where he toils.

DEVON FALLS.

CHAPTER XIII.

FROM DIMBULA TO NUWARA ELIYA.

WE are still in the district of Dimbula, and it will be remembered that we left the railway at Talawakelle. To this place we now return; but before we proceed by rail through upper Dimbula we will take a drive of a couple of miles to Devon estate, where one of the most beautiful landscapes in Ceylon is to be found. We have already seen the S. Clair Falls; but we pass them again on the winding road which leads us to Devon estate; and then, after proceeding half a mile farther, the lofty cataract known as Devon Falls bursts into view as we round an abrupt corner of the road. No photograph can do it justice; the charm of the view is in the setting of the waterfall with its steep and rugged background of rock, and the estates at various elevations towering above it, while the more distant ridges one by one recede till the farthermost is lost in rolling vapours. There are here five miles of road that present some exquisite landscapes seldom seen by the visitor, who usually pushes on with all speed to Nuwara Eliya. Thither we will now go; but we shall find much to interest us during the final ascent to Nanu Oya, as we wind about the mountain sides through Upper Dimbula. We take train again at Tallawakelle, and after a mile or two a distant view of the beautiful Devon Falls is noticed. An interesting feature of this part of the journey is the curious serpentine winding of the line. In one place to advance a single furlong it takes a curve of nearly a mile in length, tracing the outline of a huge soda-water bottle, and rising meanwhile ninety feet. The windings necessary to reach the Great Western mountains now become so compressed that to accomplish the distance of about one mile direct the train traverses six miles of railway in a fashion so circuitous that a straight line drawn from a certain point would cross the rails nine times. We cannot without wearisome tautology continue a verbal description of tea estates; but it will not be amiss to look at them in silence as we pass through this very important and beautiful district. A few views are therefore introduced with a word or two only of explanation.

Our first view looks across Upper Dimbula from the road below Nanu Oya. We see the hill-sides everywhere covered with tea, while in the distance towers the noble Great Western. The deep scarp between the two rows of trees near the top of the hill on the far side of the valley is the railway. If we cross over to this position and stand upon the railway line we shall obtain a view of Radella race-course. A curious and unique feature will be noticed in the rows of tea bushes which cover the ground within the course. As the coolies usually get a holiday at the time of the meeting, very animated and picturesque scenes result.

DIMBULA FROM NANU OYA.

RADELLA RACE COURSE.

ABBOTSFORD.

ROAD SCENE NEAR RADELLA.

The view of Abbotsford factory is given as a specimen of many that are situated amidst very charming surroundings, and upon sites where streams contribute place-value to the buildings. The road which we see in this picture served the district before the advent of the railway, when all the produce was carted to Nawalapitiya. It is still kept in good order, and is excellent for cycling. We give a view of this road passing by Radella.

The railway journey ends with sensational crossings upon girders laid from rock to rock over the clefts of the mountains, affording magnificent views of the Dimbula district and of Adam's Peak, twenty-five miles distant, and upwards of seven thousand feet above sea level. The lovely purple glow that softly lights the distant ridges in the early morn lends an additional charm to the return journey begun at daybreak.

While on few other railways in the world can scenes so interesting and experiences so exciting be obtained, the end is crowned by the beautiful pass between Nanu Oya and Nuwara Eliya, which is perhaps the most exquisite thing in Ceylon. In traversing its length of four and a half miles, the coach to which we must now have recourse makes a further ascent of a thousand feet. At the bottom of the ravine, bordered by tree ferns innumerable, the Nanu Oya River is seen foaming amongst its huge boulders, and the brilliant trees of the primæval forest in various stages of growth, marked in this land of no seasons by tints of scarlet, gold, crimson, sallow green, and, most striking of all, the rich claret colour, the chief glory of the Keena tree. Here is no leafless winter, though we have reached

IN THE NANU OYA PASS.

an altitude where frost is not unknown. In such a climate, however, with bright, warm and sunny days following on the chilly nights, the lovely ferns, which sometimes in the early morn look so pitiable with their blackened fronds, soon recover their wonted hues.

The traveller who wishes to make the most of his opportunities should leave the coach and make his way across the narrow foot-bridge in our picture. This bridge spans the Nanu Oya just above a roaring cataract. Before the making of the road and the construction of the bridges, horsemen used to cross at this point upon the rocks that here strew the river bed, a practice not unattended with risk, as was proved a few years ago by the fatal accident to a planter, whose horse stumbled upon a boulder and fell with his rider over the cataract. Below the fall is a succession of dells and dingles, the favourite haunts of picnic parties from Nuwara Eliya.

The road through this pass is of recent construction, and was made to connect Nuwara Eliya with the railway at Nanu Oya. At about the fourth mile of our coach drive we come to the final reach of the pass, and here we are again in the midst of tea, passing through the famous Scrubs Estate of the Ceylon Tea Plantations Company. The highest point of cultivation on this property is seven thousand feet above sea level; but notwithstanding the cold nights and occasional frosts at this lofty elevation the hardy little tea shrub accommodates itself to the extremes and variations of temperature, and yields the very satisfactory quantity of six hundred and fifty pounds of made tea to the acre. It is, moreover, of remarkably fine quality, and always commands a good price. We notice the factory of this estate on the right of our picture. Here visitors to Nuwara Eliya are welcomed and have the privilege not only of seeing teas made, but of purchasing them on the spot, where their purity can be assured. The convenience of such purchases being forwarded to any address in the world, payment being deferred until delivery, is one that cannot well be over-estimated.

Before we emerge upon the plain of Nuwara Eliya the features of the landscape from the top of the pass will arrest our attention for a moment. The altitude which we have reached is 6,200 feet, and as we look back and around we notice many forest-capped mountains that rise still higher. These are Kuduhugalla, 7,607 feet above sea level; Totapella, 7,746 feet; and Kirigalpotta, which reaches to the height of 7,832 feet. This strange name owes its origin to a white rock at the summit in the form of an open book, the literal translation of "Kirigalpotta" being "milk-stone-book-Mountain." Much of the forest on these lofty mountains would be cleared and the land brought under cultivation but for the resolution of late years adopted by the government to sell no land above the altitude of five thousand feet. The risk of reducing the rainfall by the destruction of forest is the obvious justification of this resolve. We have now reached Nuwara Eliya, which we have called "the playground of Ceylon, and we shall here discuss the recreations of the European colonist. Each planting district has its social and athletic clubs, and in some instances its race-course too. We have noticed Radella race-course amongst the tea in Dimbula, and

THE SCRUBS ESTATE.

we have seen many lawn-tennis and croquet courts as we have passed through the various districts; but it will suffice to deal with this part of our subject in connection with one district only, and for our purpose Nuwara Eliya will be found suitable. But it is not for recreation alone that Nuwara Eliya exists, and our next chapter will be devoted to all its features.

CHAPTER XIV.

NUWARA ELIYA.

THERE is probably no other place in the world that possesses such a remarkable combination of attractions as Nuwara Eliya and its surrounding districts. This fact should be noted by that large class of our countrymen who winter abroad. Seven thousand miles from London, six degrees from the equator, and 6,200 feet above the sea, lies this unique retreat, whose precious attributes, not long ago inaccessible, are fast becoming familiar to thousands, and especially to the ever-increasing army of wanderers who flee from the rigours of the European winter.

Egypt has its healing climate, the Engadine its lovely scenery, Brazil its wooded wilderness, the Alps their flowery meadows, and Peru its high plateau; but here, in one of our own colonies, easy of access and free from any serious drawback, are all these and a hundred other attractions, forming a combination of the most delightful conditions under which man can desire to live.

In the West Highlands of Scotland, both landscape and climate, at their best, may be suggestive of Nuwara Eliya, but the latter has a special charm of

ENTRANCE TO NUWARA ELIYA FROM THE RAMBODDE PASS.

situation which, as we shall see, possesses advantages over every other health resort in the world. Here we can enjoy the purest and most invigorating air, with a temperature best suited to the health of Europeans, and yet look down upon a luxuriant tropical country at our feet. We can experience the change from a glorious bright day to a cold Scotch mist, and yet, if we choose, we can leave the moist atmosphere and leaden sky at will, and by an hour's walk reach dry hills and sunny plains.

A clear idea of the situation of this favoured spot can best be gained by regarding the highlands of Ceylon as one huge upheaval, having an area of about 4,000 square miles, with an irregular surface of hills and peaks of varying elevation, deep ravines and grassy plains, dense forests and open valleys, gentle streams and roaring cataracts; a dozen distinct climates, each with its special characteristics of animal and vegetable life, from the lofty palms and gorgeous flowering shrubs of the lower elevations to the hardwood trees and English flowers of the highest; from the steaming haunts of the bear and buffalo to the cool regions beloved of the elk and elephant. There are choice of climate and choice of scenery to suit any constitution and to gratify every taste; the wildest rugged country and the sweetest undulating grassy plains; wild sport for the daring, golf-links and trout-fishing for quieter spirits, and a new world withal for those who need a complete change from familiar scenes.

From the base of this mighty upheaval rise abruptly the four extensive ledges which we observed from the sea, at different elevations, and a number of lofty mountains, some of which reach the height of 5,000 to 8,000 feet above sea level. The highest, called Pidurutallagalla, reaches 8,280 feet, and at the foot of it lies the Nuwara Eliya plain, just 2,000 feet below. Its position is, roughly speaking, in the centre of the highlands and approximately at the highest elevation, o'ertopped by only one of the mountain ledges. What wonder, then, at its pure and unpolluted air and its marvellous effects on the enervated constitutions of denizens of the low country, who use it as a sanatorium for recruiting the energies they have lost?

And this elysium was but a few years ago the monopoly of the enterprising few. The means of access were limited to the somewhat arduous coach journey through the districts of Pussellawa and Rambodde already described. It is now accessible, even for a week-end trip, to the busy merchant on the coast; it is within easy reach of passengers who call at the port of Colombo *en route* for other countries, and, as we have already hinted, it is deserving the attention of the European invalid in search of winter quarters. Not only have the recent extensions of the Ceylon Government Railway rendered the journey easy, cheap, and luxurious, but a new district has been reached little inferior to Nuwara Eliya itself, and having the same health-giving characteristics. This is the adjoining district of Uva, which is always fine when Nuwara Eliya is wet, whereas Nuwara Eliya is generally fine when Uva is wet. Thus can the holiday-maker always obtain fine weather without risk or delay. Details of this curious phenomenon will be given later.

To the newly-arrived visitor nothing is more astonishing than the mental and physical change

"A PURLING STREAM BABBLES THROUGH THE VALLEY" (*see page* 215).

that he himself experiences. The pale and languid victim of the sultry plains is surprised at the sudden return of his lost appetite and the delightful glow that pervades the system, marking the return of the warm tints of health. A few days effect a still greater change; the muscles become firm, the limbs gain vigour, and, above all, the rising spirits rapidly dispel the clouds of depression and invest existence with new delight. All this is due to the wonderful influence of the pure mountain air. Such was the experience of Sir Samuel Baker, the mighty hunter and explorer, so far back as fifty years ago. After shooting in the lowlands for about a year he was attacked by jungle fever and reduced to a mere shadow. As soon as he was able to endure the journey he was sent by his doctor to Nuwara Eliya. What better testimony of its invigorating influence is needed than this? "A poor and miserable wretch I was upon my arrival at this elevated station, suffering not only from the fever itself but from the feeling of an exquisite debility that creates an utter hopelessness of the renewal of strength. I was only a fortnight at Nuwara Eliya. The rest-house was the perfection of everything that was dirty and uncomfortable. The toughest possible specimen of a beefsteak, black bread and potatoes, were the choicest and only viands obtainable for an invalid. There was literally nothing else; it was a land of starvation. But the climate! What can I say to describe the wonderful effects of such a pure and unpolluted air? Simply, that at the expiration of a fortnight, in spite of the tough beef and the black bread and potatoes, I was as well and as strong as I ever had been; and in proof of this, I started instanter for another shooting excursion in the interior."

When we remember that Nuwara Eliya is only six degrees north of the equator, and no more than 6,240 feet above the sea, the mean temperature, which is only 57° Fahrenheit, appears extraordinarily low. There is no doubt that this is mainly due to the geographical position of the island. Its moderate dimensions expose it to the full influence of the surrounding seas, with their uniform temperature, while it is subject to the direct rays of the sun only twelve hours out of the twenty-four. The intense evaporation by day and the rapid cooling by night are also two important factors in the climatic peculiarities of the island.

Not the least among the features that contribute to the growing popularity of Nuwara Eliya is the appeal to the inveterate instincts of the Northman, who has so large a share in that composite being the true Briton. Though there is no winter in Ceylon, he still has a hankering after a fire on his hearth and a blanket on his bed. These delights, unknown in Colombo, can be enjoyed and appreciated at Nuwara Eliya, and in them he finds the satisfaction of a natural instinct and a reminiscence of his northern home.

Nuwara Eliya is an elliptical mountain valley, the plateau being 6,240 feet above sea level and about eight miles in circumference. It is surrounded by steep mountain ridges rising to a height varying from a few hundred to two thousand feet above the plain. There are four gaps—that on the north-east leading into the Kotmalé valley, that on the south-east to the province of Uva, that on the

"NUWARA ELIYA IS SURROUNDED BY STEEP MOUNTAIN RIDGES."

"WATER OF UNIMPEACHABLE PURITY FLOWS FROM THE HEIGHTS."

west to the Dimbula valley, and that on the east to Kandapolla and Udapussellawa. The tops themselves are for the most part thickly wooded, and still constitute favourite haunts of the leopard, the elk, and the elephant, not to mention such small deer as monkeys, who swarm in troops through the forests. The plain is charmingly undulated, and, owing nothing to cultivation, forms an admirable playground for both residents and visitors. In this connection it boasts, like so many others, of the best golf links out of Scotland, and possesses an excellent race-course. It is for the most part clear of timber, with the exception of great numbers of fine rhododendron trees, which grow freely everywhere, not as moderate bushes such as we see in England, but as large forest trees, sometimes to a height of sixty feet, with gnarled stems five feet in girth. Though only of one species (*Rhododendron arboreum*), there are two varieties, one bearing scarlet and the other pink blossoms. It is a grand sight in the month of May to see a forest of these trees, then at the height of their glory, and some of them more than one hundred years old, with their lofty branches as full of flowers as are the twigs of the modest bushes that are regarded as such a feature of Richmond Park or Kew.

The bungalows of the residents are mostly built upon grassy knolls at the foot of the mountains, and are surrounded by choice gardens not unfrequently bordered by hedgerows of geraniums. Water of unimpeachable purity flows from the heights over picturesque waterfalls of great beauty. A purling stream babbles through the middle of the valley, finally losing itself in a lake which is surrounded by a well-constructed carriage drive six miles in length. From the Grand Hotel looking east the landscape appears as represented by our photograph. The points of interest portrayed are the *Lobelia Excelsa*, growing in wild profusion to the right of the wild and uncultivated foreground, the Gregory lake, the famous Hakgalla, or "mouth rock," fully six miles distant, and the cloud effect, which is a distinctive feature of the remarkable phenomenon of the alternative climate to which brief reference has already been made.

The existence of these two distinct and separate climates is due to the action of the trade winds conditioned by the peculiar formation of the mountain district, and the effect is this: When Nuwara Eliya is basking in fine weather and bright sunshine, storm-clouds and rain cover the districts beyond the rock shown in our picture, and *vice versâ*. So sharp is the boundary that during the rainy season at Nuwara Eliya a clear sky and sunny weather can always be obtained by an hour's drive into the district of Uva. The effects produced by the masses of cloud that constantly hover above the Hakgalla rock are grand in the extreme. The graceful forms evolved out of the mists as they roll onwards from the east till they approach the Nuwara Eliya range are not the least beautiful of the natural characteristics of the place.

Although this astonishing effect is not limited to the immediate neighbourhood of Hakgalla, but extends to the whole range, yet from the plateau this towering rock, with its forest-clad slopes and its precipitous eastern shoulder of more than a thousand feet sheer descent, seems alone to rule

"THE GRACEFUL FORMS EVOLVED OUT OF THE MISTS AS THEY ROLL ONWARDS FROM THE EAST."

the storms, and to check them in their headlong struggle to reach the sunny plain, holding them in ever fearful obedience; season after season the wind may howl and the forests groan, but past the rock they never come. The hither side is the reserve of storm-clouds from the west, which, when the south-west monsoon sets in, form up in the same majestic array upon the whole western side of the ridge, leaving the eastern clear and resplendent with sunshine. But upon approaching Hakgalla from the west we reverse the picture. The clouds dissolve into a thick mist, which fills the lovely gorge between the opposing slopes. Onwards the traveller wends his way till, as through a veil, he sees at his feet the charming panorama of Uva glistening beneath a cloudless sky. A few more minutes and he treads the dusty road, while behind him a rainbow may be seen almost encircling the veil of mist which now enshrouds the hills he has left.

This choice of climate is now available at all seasons in consequence of the recent extension of the railway into the heart of the Uva district, and Bandarawella, commanding the most beautiful prospect in this region, might well become the sanatorium of Ceylon while Nuwara Eliya is under its rainy mantle; already an hotel has been opened there by the company that provides for our comfort at the latter place. But let it not be supposed that the merits of Nuwara Eliya as a health resort disappear with the fine weather. It is true that during the second half of the year rainy days are prevalent, but the occasional bright spells intervening bring the most glorious days of the year, and the worst that can be said is that during this period it resembles a rather wet summer in the Highlands of Scotland. Moderately warm days, with a Scotch mist, followed by cool evenings that allure to the cheerful fireside of a well-furnished and carpeted bungalow, with intermittent days of sunshine, and a change to any temperate climate you may fancy within easy distance, make up a state of things not to be contemned even by those who are in a position to humour their every whim.

The square plot in the middle distance in the centre of our photograph on page 217 is the tennis ground attached to St. Edward's School for European boys, the roof of which is partly visible among the trees to the left.

The foundation of this and the erection of several other buildings must have been a considerable gratification to the late Sir Samuel Baker, who upon his arrival in Nuwara Eliya nearly half a century ago, wrote: "Why should not the highlands of Ceylon, with an Italian climate, be rescued from this state of barrenness? . . . Why should not schools be established, a comfortable hotel erected, a church built?" These and many other excellent institutions are now well established. In place of the uncomfortable rest-house, with its rather monotonous *menu* of tough beef and black bread, there are hotels whose extensive grounds abound with romantic nooks interesting alike to the artist and the man of science.

"THE LAKE OF NUWARA ELIYA IS SURROUNDED BY A CARRIAGE DRIVE SIX MILES IN LENGTH."

CHAPTER XV.

PIDURUTALLAGALLA.

THERE is perhaps nothing more attractive to the traveller who visits Nuwara Eliya than a walk to the summit of Pidurutallagalla, the highest mountain in the island. The ascent is easy, and the reward great. From no other mountain top in the world can you literally see over a whole island of such extent and beauty as you can from this. From shore to shore lie outstretched in every direction forests and plains, mountain ranges interlaced in intricate confusion, masses of verdant patana lands, interspersed with glittering streams; while the stillness of the profound solitude is only broken by the sounds from mountain torrents in their wild rush over the huge boulders in the rocky ravines. It is here, with the accumulated impressions of the whole journey from the coast to the highest point of the highlands fresh in his mind, that the traveller confers on Ceylon the title of "the show place of the universe."

The journey to the top is about four miles, and a very good two and a half hours' walk. There is also a choice between covering the whole distance on horseback and being carried on the shoulders of four coolies in a chair supported on two bamboo poles; the latter method, however, although frequently adopted by ladies, is not too comfortable, especially when the coolies are of unequal height. In any case the ground is so uneven, that it is impossible to keep the bamboos in a horizontal position. The glorious exhilaration of the pure and bracing air encourages residents in Nuwara Eliya to make frequent excursions on this account alone. The prospect varies so much under different atmospheric conditions that every fresh trip is amply rewarded by the everchanging scenes that meet the gaze, while the cloud studies surpass even those of Alpine countries.

But grandest of all is that beautiful scene which heralds the approach of day. To stand upon the highest point of this sea-girt land, with the shadowed sky above and brooding darkness below, there to watch the rosy-fingered dawn cast her first rays upon the thousand peaks that begin to peep through the snowy mists which yet enshroud the low-lying valleys, is an experience well worth the surrender of a few hours of sleep and an occasional fright at midnight forest sounds betokening the proximity of some denizen of the jungle. The first glimmer of light reveals snowy masses of mist as far as the eye can scan, right away to the ocean east and west, with lighted peaks peering through the veil resembling laughing islands dotting a sea of foam. Then as the dawn breaks a golden tint gradually appears over the hills, and when the sun bursts over the horizon, a rapid transformation takes place. The petrified surf of the mists now begins to move upwards, and reveals with vivid clearness the valleys all fresh from their repose. The dewy leaves of the forest trees and the trails of beautiful moss which cling to their branches glisten with tints of gold, the moistened rocks sparkle with diamonds, and all nature rejoices at the new-born day.

As the sun rises higher the nearer slopes become more distinct, and the distant ranges clearly visible right away to Adam's Peak, The intermediate ranges of the Great Western (7,264 feet), five miles west of Nuwara Eliya, to which reference has already been made in a previous chapter, and Talankanda range (6,137 feet), dividing the tea-growing districts of Dimbula and Dickoya, are seen most clearly as the rays of the sun increase.

Nuwara Eliya is lying at our feet. The whole plain glistens with hoar frost or sparkling dew; the river, like a silver streak, winds its course to the Hakgalla gorge, and for a great distance ranges of forest-clad mountains alternate with waving plains. The nearest range is that called after One Tree Hill, then comes the Elk Plains range, the next is a mountain of the Agra Patana district, and the lofty range in the distance is that of Horton Plains. The tops of all these ranges are clothed with forests, while undulating patanas cover the ridges between.

Upon these forest clad mountains the elk abounds, and at night in great numbers swoops down upon the bungalow gardens, destroying the fences and eating the vegetables. It is difficult to hunt these animals, not only on account of the depth of the forest, but also of the interference of leopards with the sport, in which the dogs come upon the latter, give tongue and chase, and receive a pat on the head, which puts a sudden end to their

P

career. The nocturnal depredations of the leopard being limited to the occasional theft of a cow from the compound are of much less concern than those of the more destructive elk.

As we descend by the broadening day we notice the great contrast between the character of the Pidurutallagalla forest and that of the lowlands. Instead of waving palms we see weird trees with gnarled trunks and forked boughs, festooned with long beards of lichens and orange moss. Many of the trunks are clothed with rich green creepers and adorned with the fantastic blossoms of native orchids, and parasites innumerable bedeck the upper branches with strangest flowers, while the magnificent *Rhododendron arboreum*, with its great branches and brilliant blossoms, appears everywhere as a common forest tree.

The creatures of the mountain summits being nocturnal in their habits, there are no outward signs of life by day, deep silence taking the place of the noise that proceeds from the thickets of the low country plains. The elephant and the leopard are seldom seen or heard, but remain hidden in the deepest recesses. A couple of large wanderoo monkeys may sometimes be seen quarrelling like angry school boys; but as a rule the only sound is the occasional deep note of the jungle cock, and even he is so modest in hiding his brilliant plumage from the eye of man that he seldom falls a victim to the sportsman's gun.

In the garden of Keena Hotel, at the foot of the mountain, stands a solitary Keena tree whose gnarled stem measures thirty-five feet at its base and twenty-six feet when measured fifty-four inches from the ground, and has withstood the blasts of a hundred monsoons; but its once beautiful crown, changing its tints from green to a rich red, according to the season of the year, is gradually disappearing. Fifteen years ago, when the author was tenant of this house as a private residence, its downward course had scarce begun, but here, as elsewhere, death marks his victims, and a dozen more years may

THE MONARCH OF THE KEENAS.

see the final doom of this well-known monarch of the Keenas.

Of this tree there are no less than twelve varieties in Ceylon. It grows in all the mountain forests above an altitude of three thousand feet. The wood is of dark red colour, and being very hard, weather-proof, and durable, is much used for the roofing of bungalows.

CHAPTER XVI.

GENERAL FEATURES OF NUWARA ELIYA.

FREEDOM to roam at will in his native land is a privilege seldom enjoyed by an Englishman. The restrictions imposed by private ownership are one of the greatest drawbacks to life in the old country; and the absence of these restrictions in Nuwara Eliya invests it with a special charm. The resident or the visitor can practically set his foot anywhere he pleases. Not even the tea and other estates need be excepted, for their owners welcome all who care to make use of their private roads to display their interest in the cultivation of the various products.

An easy stroll of two miles brings us to the top of Naseby Hill, commanding a wonderful view of the principal peaks of the island. On a clear day both Adam's Peak and Namunakulakanda are both distinctly visible, although distant from each other forty-seven miles in a direct line. But the chief feature is the charming character of the scenery immediately surrounding the tea plantation which encircles the hill.

On the west the calm waters of the lake reflecting the wooded hills and the lofty mountains, recall memories of Ullswater.

"THE CALM WATERS OF THE LAKE REFLECTING THE WOODED HILLS."

On the east is the precipitous shoulder of Pidurutallagalla, known as Lovers' Leap, taking its name from the legend that tells how a Kandyan prince became greatly attached to a maiden of low caste. Upon the fact coming to the King's knowledge, the lovers took to flight, and were pursued by the King's soldiers to the mountain range of Pidurutallagalla. Seeing no hope of escape, they preferred to be united in death rather than in life to be divided, and in sight of their pursuers, locked in a last embrace, leapt from this precipice.

From Naseby we see the best outline of Hakgalla, and obtain many pretty peeps across patana and forest in the direction of the Moon Plains. Visitors to Naseby estate are made welcome to the factory, which is a new one and fitted most completely with the latest appliances for the manufacture of tea; and many are the people who, when they sip the cup that cheers in the old country, think of the romantic spot where they witnessed the manufacture of the leaf that brews their favourite beverage.

Beyond Naseby is a pretty drive round the Moon Plains, so called from the number of moonstones found there. The forests are here intersected with patana, or grass land. There are various theories as to the origin of these patana lands and the distinct and sharp demarcation of the forests that bound them. There is doubtless a difference in the constituents of the patana soil and that of the forest, nevertheless it is held that the forests are encroaching upon the patana land at the rate of about a yard in a year. In very many cases, however, this natural extension is checked by burning off the coarse patana grass, and the consequent destruction of the young seedlings growing outside the forest edge. The long mana grass is too coarse and too deficient in nutriment to be of any value for grazing purposes, and is suitable only for thatching and litter. It has been the custom of the natives to regard the patanas as common land, and by annually firing the long grass they obtain young shoots for their cattle. Even these young shoots, however, are poor stuff for this purpose, and it is considered that nothing short of scientific farming can render the soil of any service. That it can be cultivated has been abundantly proved. Some of the best tea in the Udapussellawa and other districts has been grown by careful treatment upon patana land. It is difficult to see why the Government, interested as it is in the increase of the mountain forests, should not secure their gradual extension by protecting the patanas, and in the course of time sell portions of the older forests, where the soil is suitable for tea cultivation. The road round the Moon Plains and across these patanas brings us to a magnificent ravine, five hundred feet sheer down from the road. This is the most beautifully wooded mountain gorge in the district. We next come upon the Barrack Plains Lake, which, owing to the hills that surround it, resembles a loch of the Scotch Highlands. Although there are rivers innumerable, expanses of water are very rare in the highlands of Ceylon, notwithstanding the great need of them.

Before we can be said to have taken a complete survey of the general features of Nuwara Eliya we must take a walk to the top of the northern gap or entrance to the Rambodde pass. It is best for

THE BARRACK PLAINS LAKE.

our purpose to walk, because such are the intricate windings of the road that in rapid locomotion our attention is apt to be diverted from the landscape to the dangers of our immediate position. The golf links are first seen on our right, and on the left the pretty grounds of the Governor's residence. Thence we ascend by a steep gradient until we reach the point of vantage depicted in our photograph on page 205.

There are various theories by which it is sought to prove that in the remote past Nuwara Eliya was a thickly populated and very important station, though all we really know is that a century ago it was uninhabited. Its re-discovery is due to the enterprise of Dr. Davy, a brother of the celebrated Sir Humphry, who made his way thither in 1819. A portion of his own account is worth quoting here. He says: "We entered a forest, in which we began to see traces of elephants, and proceeded over wooded hills, gradually descending till we came to a great extent of open country, the aspect of which was no less novel than agreeable. Our guides called it Neuraelliyapattan. In point of elevation and extent, this tract, there is reason to believe, surpasses every other of the kind in the island; perhaps it is fifteen or twenty miles in circumference, and its average height may be about 5,300 feet above the level of the sea. Surrounded by the tops of mountains, which have the appearance of hills of moderate height, its character is that of table-land, elevated and depressed into numerous hillocks and hollows. The wood which covers the boundary mountains (and they are all, without exception, covered with wood) is of a peculiar kind, quite Alpine. The same kind of wood ramifying into the table-land, and occurring scattered about in insulated clumps, with large solitary rhododendrons here and there, has a very picturesque effect, and helps to make a very charming landscape. Beautiful as this region is, and cleared, and possessing, in all probability, a fine climate (certainly a cool climate), it is quite deserted by man. It is the dominion entirely of wild animals; and, in an especial manner, of the elephant, of whom we saw innumerable traces."

There are signs visible around Nuwara Eliya of an ancient irrigation system, which must have involved immense labour and great engineering skill. These seem to demand the theory of former prosperity and immense population. Sir Samuel Baker thought that the supposed ancient importance of the place was due to its sources of water supply, upon which the lower regions depended, and to its gems. Traces of masonry in the angles of ravines suggest that the watercourses were at one time very numerous, and that they were directed to vast stretches of country now cultivated and covered with jungle. Most of these courses are now dry, and the gigantic aqueducts of two thousand years ago are overgrown with forest trees. There are remains of one impressive work of masonry, apparently unfinished, about which a Singhalese legend says that it was begun one early morning by a giant, who at mid-day, hearing of the illness of his wife, left his work and never returned.

But whatever may have been its glorious past—and the extensive ruins in the North Central Province prove beyond question that the country was thickly populated before the Christian era—we owe its present usefulness as a sanatorium in the first place to the efforts of a remarkable man, the road-maker of the century, and in the next to the extension of the Government railway.

Major Skinner arrived in Ceylon in the year 1814, at the age of fourteen, at a time when the journey from Colombo to Kandy, across swamps, jungle, and ravines, occupied about six weeks. Two years after his arrival young Skinner was entrusted by the Governor, Sir Edward Barnes, with the construction of a most difficult part of a road, which was soon to bring this hitherto almost inaccessible region within five days' march of Colombo. To the genius of this lad the success of the enterprise was mainly due. Becoming an officer of the Ceylon Rifles, he soon applied military organisation to the work for which his abilities so obviously fitted him by enlisting a pioneer force to the number of about four thousand men, in order that he might have trained labourers on whom he could always rely. With an army of experienced workmen he spent nearly fifty years in the construction of roads and bridges, often undergoing the greatest privations during his surveys of the trackless wilderness. Few men have left behind them such an imperishable record of a useful career as the accomplished and unassuming Major Skinner. The magnificent network of roads all over the country is his lasting memorial. Upon his arrival there were none, and at his departure there were three thousand miles, mostly due to his genius, pluck, energy, and self-reliance.

We have now some idea of the general features of this district, and it has doubtless suggested sport to our minds. We will therefore pursue this subject before we discuss life and recreations generally at the sanatorium.

"BELTS OF FOREST SEPARATE THE EXTENSIVE PLAINS OF PATANA." (SEE PAGE 2

"ONWARDS AMONGST THE HUGE BOULDERS THAT STREW THE DEPTHS OF THE GORGES."

CHAPTER XVII.

SPORT.

THE facility with which the regions of wild game are now reached has not yet succeeded in depriving the island of its claim to be regarded as a sporting country. It has always been celebrated for its elephants, leopards, elk, bears, buffalo, and hogs; and although the ruthless slaughter which is carried on by the natives, even during the close season from May to October, has undoubtedly reduced their numbers in recent years, there is still a large amount of game, and as no period of protection is afforded the leopard, bear, or elephant, the visitor who has a taste for hunting can be suited all the year round.

Perhaps the best sport which Nuwara Eliya affords is that of Sambur hunting in the belts of forest which separate the extensive plains of patana or grass land. Those who have read Sir Samuel Baker's graphic descriptions of elk hunting in this neighbourhood may be told that the same sport is being enjoyed in this year 1900. The thrilling incidents which he described in the fifties are ours to-day, and we realise as we come across the same scenes and situations how faithful his descriptions were:

deep ravines with their rugged cliffs of gneiss rock, rivers dashing over precipices and onwards in great commotion amongst the huge boulders that strew the depths of the gorges, a boundless panorama of beautiful hunting country with unnumbered obstructions and dangers that give zest to the sport; elk abounding in the forests that cover the summits of the mountains, and ever ready to bound across the steep and rugged grass lands when disturbed by the hounds—they are the same to-day.

The meet is early: usually at six. In such a country horses are useless, and the sportsman, who must be in good training, follows the hounds on foot through jungle and river, across mountain and plain, with knife in hand. This is his only weapon for every emergency, and although the sambur deer or elk, as he is locally called, is the animal sought, the dogs may at any moment give tongue to the ferocious and more dangerous boar. When the elk is found he makes for the nearest water, even though it be miles distant, through tangled jungle, steep ravines and trackless forests, followed by the hounds, who almost out-distance the huntsmen; the latter strive for the foremost place, and the first man who comes up with the stag at bay has the honour of knifing him, a task which requires considerable skill and agility.

The chase is an almost everyday affair. I was out this morning in company with my two daughters, keener on the sport than I. We left the bungalow at 5.30 a.m., while the air was keen and frosty, and the first gleams of golden light were appearing in the eastern sky. Mounting our bicycles we wheeled speedily through the light mountain atmos-

"ONWARDS UP THE NEXT STEEP AND DOWN AGAIN WE RAN."

phere, clear, cold and inspiriting. As we sped round the lake Pidurutallagalla was magnificently reflected upon its still, smooth surface. We passed the very spot where Baker's pack was kennelled nearly fifty years ago, and where the mighty hunter himself dwelt for some years. Another mile brought us to the Sita Ellia plains. Here our cycles were left in the forest, and trusting henceforth to our legs we doubled over the rough patanas to the music of the pack, already on the track of a fine buck. The long grass was sparkling with dew, and the tufts in which it grows soon occasioned a few headlong falls as in wild excitement we scaled the steep ascent. Soon we reached the scene depicted by our photograph, and for a moment caught a glimpse of the hounds bounding from the forest; then we lost sight of them in the distance, which we knew by the music was gradually increasing. To follow now became a matter of difficulty. Between the knoll on which we stood and the distant patanas was a stream with steep banks. Away we went, running when we could and at other times sliding in a sitting posture. In the latter attitude we descended into the stream, and in our excitement we did not even remark upon the icy coldness of the water. Onwards up the next steep and down again we ran till at length we came to a long and narrow wooded ravine. Now we could hear distinct signals that our game was at bay far away up the stream. The locality was, however, so densely wooded that there was no possibility of our seeing the capture except by choosing the river bed for our path. Fortunately the water was scarcely knee-deep, and so into it we sprang. After wading up stream for a quarter of a mile we were just in time to see the bay and the end of the fine fellow as he was knifed by one of the huntsmen who had arrived by another route. The find and the kill were quicker than usual, but it gave us some vigorous exercise and we returned to breakfast thoroughly mud-stained from head to foot; but with appetites as rude as could possibly be desired.

The best hunting is to be had on the Horton Plains, distant from Nuwara Eliya about sixteen miles, and seven thousand feet above sea level. Until the recent railway extension these wilds were so isolated from human interference that the elk, red deer, wild boar, and leopard dwelt there in almost excessive numbers, and the sportsmen of Ceylon could always depend upon a good bag. The rest-house which we illustrate was the only building for fifteen miles, and it was chiefly used by hunting and shooting parties. It is still the resort of sportsmen, and although it can accommodate a goodly number, the improved means of access and the introduction of trout into the streams that flow through the plains has so much increased the number of visitors that additions of considerable extent are about to be made.

The famous abyss known as "the world's end" also attracts a number of travellers. This merits a few lines of description. The southern portion of the great table-land ends so abruptly as to give the sensation of having literally arrived at the end of the world. The traveller comes upon this suddenly when emerging from the forest, and the effect is startling in the extreme. To approach to the very edge of the giddy precipice is a trial for the

"NO CHOICE BUT THE RIVER-BED FOR OUR PATH."

HORTON PLAINS RESTHOUSE

WHERE THE STAG COMES TO BAY

strongest nerve, but securely fastened to a tree by a rope round the waist one may stand at the brink and gaze straight down the sheer side of the mountain upon another world five thousand feet below, and even hurl down a huge boulder without a sound returning from the crash of its contact with the earth. Here is an atmosphere bracing and cold: there lie the steaming plains of the low country. Behind lies a wild and almost unfrequented region, while below nestle the cosy bungalows of the Balangoda district, in the midst of expanses of tea bushes, only 1,700 feet above sea level. Such is the distance of the plantations, rivers, bungalows, and forests, that only by the aid of a telescope can the nature of any particular object be determined. Few human eyes looked across that marvellous abyss until quite recent years; but with the facilities now offered by the railway it is becoming a more frequented spot. Although the leopard may have deserted his old lair and the herds of elephants betaken themselves to quieter regions undisturbed by the iron horse, the same weird forests, with their dense undergrowth of masses of nelu scrub, the same magnificent landscapes and the impressive scene at the "World's End" are there unaltered. Few people now journey to the Horton Plains by the old paths from Nuwara Eliya, and they will therefore soon be overgrown and effaced, while the crossings over streams and gullies will decay and perish. It is now usual to go to Nana Oya by coach, and thence to proceed up the Bandarawela railway to Ohiya. From Ohiya the entrance to the plains may be reached by a climb of about an hour and a half over rugged country, and the return journey is now best made by the old Nuwara Eliya path for about eight miles to Ambawela, and thence by rail to Nana Oya. By this route very grand views of scenery from the side of the Totapola range may be obtained, and many delightful bits of forest, differing in character from any elsewhere. The trees, which look so old and undisturbed with their rich long beards of variegated moss, appeared to be dwarfed by the cold of their lofty and exposed situation. Wild flowers, orchids, and ferns always render the scene fairy-like in the sunshine, but it is when the nelu is in blossom that these highland forests transcend in beauty almost every other part of Ceylon. This lovely flowering shrub, of the *Strobilanthes* family, is the chief undergrowth in these forests, and the species number as many as twenty-seven, some of which grow only in the drier parts of the country, but about twenty of them favour those forests with a considerable rainfall. Some are delicate and small, others have thick cane stems and grow to a great height. The blossoms cluster round the joints of their stems, and display great variety of colour—blue, purple, red, white, and the parti-coloured crimson and white. The blossoming is so profuse that the plant takes some years to recover, and it is therefore seldom that these high jungles are seen in their fullest glory. The fragrance of the atmosphere is no less remarkable than the beauty of the scene. Huge swarms of bees are attracted by the flowers, and when these are succeeded by the nuts, all sorts of creatures appear, as if by magic, to take their turn at the feast.

Coming down the side of Totapola, we obtain grand views of Nuwara Eliya, a thousand feet below; even its bungalows and lake being dis-

"THE TREES WHICH LOOK SO OLD AND UNDISTURBED, WITH THEIR RICH LONG BEARDS OF VARIEGATED MOSS."

tinctly visible on a clear day, though twelve miles distant.

The best districts for shooting lie within a day or two's journey from Nuwara Eliya ; Hambantotte, on the west coast, being perhaps the most favoured by sportsmen. Here the game consists chiefly of bear, buffalo, and elephant, all of which are numerous in that part of the country, but more especially the first, who may be met with near any water-hole. Smaller game is very plentiful, comprising chiefly the tiger-cat, monkey, porcupine, and crocodile ; while among the birds are peafowl, jungle fowl, flamingoes, pelicans, cranes, snipe, and quail.

We shall make some further observations on this subject when we visit Trincomali and other places famous for sport ; but at present this brief description may serve to show that in spite of the rapid spread of cultivation since the days of such giants of the rifle as Sir Samuel Baker and Major Rogers, the sportsman is still well catered for, and that the island even yet provides plenty of all descriptions of sport, in comparison with which those of the old country seem tame in the extreme.

GOLF CADDIE.

CHAPTER XVIII.

LIFE IN NUWARA ELIYA.

THE European population of Nuwara Eliya numbers about three hundred, many of whom are all the year round residents having estates in the district, and others who for the most part, having their occupations in Colombo or other towns of the low country, still possess the luxury of a residence at the Sanatorium, which they usually occupy in "the season."

Most of these residences are built after the bungalow style with only ground floor, but since the present Governor of the Colony, The Right Honourable Sir J. West Ridgeway, gave his hearty support to the development of the station as a sanatorium, there has been an increased demand for building sites and a decided improvement in the character of the buildings. The fashion for two stories and some regard for architectural design is gaining ground. The best available sites are government land, which may be purchased for building purposes upon favourable terms. It is therefore not unlikely that the two hundred or so bungalows which now dot the hill-sides will ere long be doubled in number. Moreover, a branch line of railway from Nanu Oya to

Udapussellawa is soon to cross the plain, and, although we do not welcome this from an æsthetic point of view, it will doubtless increase the number of residents and visitors.

As in all eastern towns the native population has its own quarter, which is as compact as that of the Europeans is scattered. The domestic servants, who provide their own food, and many of whom have families, contribute very largely to the native

NATIVES AT THE JYMKHANA.

population and the support of the native bazaars. The total native population of Nuwara Eliya cannot be less than two thousand five hundred. It includes a curious admixture of Singhalese, Tamils, Moormen, Malays, and a few descendants of the Portuguese; and their professions include those of lawyers, physicians, store-keepers, astrologers, devil-dancers, pedlars, pingo-bearers, dhobies, jaggery-sellers, goldsmiths, betel-sellers, tinkers, tom-tom beaters, beggars, and others, which according to the declarations of the last census amounted to upwards of one hundred.

Although the European community is small, it cannot be said that life is in the least degree monotonous to those who are fond of country pursuits. In addition to the wild sport of the jungle, there are many distractions such as cricket, golf, polo, hockey, and lawn-tennis. The lake is full of carp, and trout have been successfully introduced into the

THE WATER JUMP.

neighbouring streams, for which licences to fish are granted for any period. The golf-links are now one of the chief attractions of the place, and are the scene of many exciting contests. There is also a well laid out race-course, and the Jymkhana is quite the event of the year. All Colombo flocks to Nuwara Eliya for the races, and the sporting fever extends even to the ladies, who vie with one another in the latest Parisian confections. Every bungalow, hotel, and club is taxed to its utmost capacity. Many who cannot find accommodation ride daily into the station, distances of twenty and even thirty miles not being considered too great even when followed by a dance at the end of the day. The invigorating mountain air seems to banish all fatigue, and nowhere is there more fun crammed into a single week than amongst the genial society and vivacious spirits to be found in Nuwara Eliya during the Jymkhana.

But of all the amusements in which Nuwara Eliya indulges we must award golf the first place, because it has the largest number of votaries and is oftenest played. That this should be so nobody wonders who sees the links and realises what a perfect golfing climate Nuwara Eliya affords. Last year there were six weeks out of the fifty-two when rain and wind seriously interfered, but for the rest of the time there was nothing to detract from the full enjoyment of the game. There are two links: one formed and used exclusively by the Nuwara Eliya Golf Club of gentlemen only, and the other a branch of the United Club for ladies and gentlemen. The former claims our attention first. It bears one great contrast to the best links in the old country in being charmingly picturesque. Its other virtues, especially its hazards, are perhaps not quite orthodox; but whatever may be implied in the term "links" as conceived by the best authorities, or required by the traditions of the game, golf in Nuwara Eliya has attractions and affords enjoyment that nowhere else can be surpassed. But it must not be supposed that I am in any way apologising for the links. It has an unusual number of river and tree hazards; but these are productive of good golf. You must

THE FIRST GREEN.

THE LINKS FROM WHITE'S FIELD

above all things be steady, straight, and consistent if you are going to hole out your full round in anything approximating Colonel Bogie's requirements. We will discuss each hole in due order, and by the aid of illustrations endeavour to give those who have not experienced the delights of golf in Nuwara Eliya some idea of the course.

Our camera being placed on the first tee and the lens directed to the first hole we obtain our view entitled "The First Green." Here we observe that there is a direct line for the putting green; but fraught with danger. At our feet there are various punishments awaiting the "top" or "foozle." The winding stream which flows to the left receives the "pull"; whins and bunkers to the right play hide and seek with the "slice." There is no mercy for the errant ball. The drive must carry the river, the near end of the foot-bridge, then the river again and the deep hollow beyond. It must be perfectly straight for the hole, and carry 160 yards before the drop if a three is to result. If it fails to carry the hollow it will probably be arrested by the steep bank. This will leave a forty yards approach requiring careful manipulation, and should result in four.

We now move off fifty yards to the left and consider the second green from its tee. Here we get a less picturesque view, but an excellent stretch of the course. The putting green 300 yards distant lies in the farthermost corner beneath the shadow of the acacias that border the road beyond. It is in a sort of basin or small gem quarry, broken away on the right side, where there is great danger from the close proximity of the river; but on the other sides it is entirely enclosed by almost precipitous banks. To get here the wide bunker which stretches across the course about one hundred yards in front of the tee must first be carried. This should leave an iron or a short "brassy" shot to the green; but it must be clean, straight, and lofted, for the green is guarded against any indifferent approach by a deep drain and steep bank. This hole is a very possible four, but should be a fairly certain five.

The third tee is within a few yards of the second hole, and the drive from it is a return journey as far as the extreme end of the bunker which we crossed from the second tee. It is 190 yards to this spot, and thence to the third hole is 169 yards. The approach is, however, fraught with dire penalties for any mistake. On our immediate right is the river and on our front is the same, while the distant green is in a sort of *cul-de-sac*, to be reached only by the straightest shot through an avenue of acacias. A mistake of any kind will render its due punishment from river, whins, or trees, and the hole, which faultless play may accomplish in four, is a very satisfactory five.

Now we turn to the right and find the fourth tee facing an almost unobstructed plain, save a deep drain that runs through the middle, and an artificial bunker; but not even here do we get any leniency towards the most ordinary mistake. The "foozle" runs into whins, the "slice" into the drain, and the "pull" over the boundary road. But a perfect drive slightly to the right of the tree visible in our picture will leave an easy approach of about eighty to one hundred yards, and thus the hole may be considered a creditable but not a difficult four.

THE FOURTH GREEN.

THE SIXTH GREEN.

The tee for the fifth green is situated in the middle distance of our picture of the fourth green; but the putting green is invisible from it. The drive is directly past the pair of acacias, which may be easily made out in the far distance, and onwards past a very treacherous corner of the bordering jungle and down a deep slope beyond. A very straight drive is essential, and should leave a short and easy approach; but a "pull" will assuredly mean lost ball in the jungle, while a "slice" will carry us into a bunker of morass. The river here flows between very steep banks near the putting green, and encourages careful approaching. The hole is a moderate four.

We are now at the extreme end of the course. In returning we make a detour for the sixth and seventh holes. Our picture is taken from a spot ten yards to the right of the tee looking direct to the sixth hole. The drive here must be straight in order to avoid the jungle on our right and a deep hollow of morass one hundred yards distant on the left. If we get away in the most desired manner we shall be confronted, in the second shot, by an artificial bunker reaching across the course. Our duty is to play a strong "brassy" to the green. This must be well aimed; for the putting green is on a peninsula, and the errant ball finds its way down a steep bank on one side or other, if not into the river. There is nothing amiss with five for this hole, but a four should be our aim.

We now play back again over the same bunker, taking a direction somewhat to the left for the seventh hole, which is on a sloping green, and should not cost more than four.

The eighth hole is reached over the same green as illustrated by our picture of the fourth. Owing to the drain, the narrow course, and the undulating putting green, this hole is a rather difficult four, and Bogey is content to do it in five.

As we mount the ninth tee a certain amount of reverential awe takes possession of us. We are perched upon a slight eminence, and a dozen possibilities of mishap confront us. What they are the reader will see by a close examination of our illustration. It must be borne in mind that the camera is upon the tee, and the foreground of the picture begins a few yards in front of it. The putting green is in the far distance between the bank of whins and the buildings. The immediate obstacles, which, however, affect only the "top" or "foozle," are clumps of furze and the river, whose banks are steep and rugged. The safest line for the drive is a fairly close proximity to the clump of trees on the left. This, however, does not always give an unobstructed approach to the green, as the distant whins guard it from this direction. Some prefer to risk a loft over this clump of acacias, which generally leaves the ball just short of a bunker and with a clear straight course to the green. The putting green, like so many of the others, is on a peninsula, and the approach therefore needs careful judgment. The hole should be accomplished in five.

At the turn the first tee again does duty for the tenth green. For some distance the river runs in a direct line for the hole, and it is wise to take a biangular course. The putting green is easily reached in two. It is visible in our picture of the links from

THE NINTH GREEN.

THE FIFTEENTH PUTTING GREEN

White's field, on page 260, and lies to the left of the second hole.

The eleventh hole is in the field from which our photograph on page 260 is taken. The drive should carry the bunker, which has been made for the protection of passengers, the road, and the hill beyond, when, if straight, it will drop in the vicinity of the green. It is a very easy four.

The twelfth hole is, like the eleventh, invisible from the tee, being in a deep hollow. A long drive of 220 yards may reach it and result in a three. It should seldom cost more than four.

The thirteenth green has no obstacle and requires only a straight drive and short approach to reach the hole. It would be an easy three, but for the fact that the putting green is a sort of inverted pudding basin guarded by a deep trench on the hither side and the river beyond.

The fourteenth putting green is within reach of the tee by a drive of one hundred and eighty-seven yards, being the shortest hole on the links. But as if to compensate for the short distance the possibilities of trouble are increased. Our photograph of the eighteenth green, on page 271, shows also the full stretch of the fourteenth. If we look for a moment at the picture we shall see the fourteenth putting green in a hollow on the right of the foreground with the river-bank in close approximation. Looking straight across the green we see a bunker in the middle distance, the tee being near the white stem of a tree visible in the far distance. It will be seen from a study of our illustration that the drive must carry the bunker; for if it is pulled to the left the ball will go into the river, and if sliced it will lie in such a position that only a too-short approach or a dead drop upon the putting green will prevent a similar catastrophe by the ball running down the river-bank beyond.

The fifteenth green is the *bête noire* of all the inexperienced or indifferent players. It affords an unobstructed drive and a very difficult approach, the latter being due to the position of the putting green, which possesses the peculiar characteristic of the Nuwara Eliya links in the highest degree—the peninsular green. We have noticed this feature at the sixth and the ninth holes, while many of the others present the same peculiarity in a lesser degree. Reference to our photograph will give a better idea than many words of description. It will be noticed that the approach which swerves in the slightest degree from the straight path will be terribly penalised; if to the left a deep ditch receives it in water; if to the right the river carries it off in rapids; and if the strength of the shot has been only a little excessive the stream receives it at the bend.

The seventeenth green is visible in our photograph on page 260. The tee is near the acacia on the extreme left; it is placed high and affords an opportunity for a magnificent drive, there being no obstruction for two hundred yards, at which distance the bunker seen in our picture is guarding the putting green.

The eighteenth green will be seen well illustrated in our photograph opposite this page. The camera is placed near the tee and looks straight for the hole, which lies beyond the whins and over the river in the middle distance. The approach is difficult and must consist of a well-judged loft dropping dead

THE EIGHTEENTH GREEN.

NUWARA ELIYA CADDIES

upon the green, which has river in front, road and ditches behind, and very rough ground on either side.

The Club consists of about four hundred members. Monthly competitions take place in addition to large meetings in January and April. No club gives a more hearty welcome to visitors, who, when introduced by two members, can use the links free for three days, or for one month upon payment of £1.

Caddies are "cheap and nasty." Threepence is a small fee as compared with the half-crown of the old country; but it must be borne in mind that the little dark brown urchins who alone are available here for this work render no service of an intelligent nature and merely save you the trouble of carrying your own bag. They are mostly small children and often o'ertopped by the clubs they carry. Considering their size and tender age their physical endurance is remarkable. The subject of our photograph on page 254 is quite equal to thirty-six holes in the day.

A considerable extension of the course is being carried out, and it is quite probable that in another year several new greens of much greater length will be available. The following table gives the distances of the holes as described above and at present (September, 1900) in use :—

1	...	220 yards.	10	...	242 yards.
2	...	301 ,,	11	...	192 ,,
3	...	359 ,,	12	...	222 ,,
4	...	258 ,,	13	...	232 ,,
5	...	236 ,,	14	...	187 ,,
6	...	363 ,,	15	...	254 ,,
7	...	224 ,,	16	...	288 ,,
8	...	330 ,,	17	...	232 ,,
9	...	298 ,,	18	...	270 ,,

Total, 4,708 yards.

As we cross the river at various points on the course many a fine trout may be seen awaiting the fly. The very successful fishing club at Nuwara Eliya is by no means the least of its attractions to visitors, who can obtain licences for the day, week or season. The club has leased from the Government the fishing rights in all waters at an elevation of over five thousand feet above sea level.

The United Club is a recent and most successful institution. It includes a Library, Reading Room, Golf Links, Croquet Courts and Lawn Tennis. Its quarters, illustrated in our photograph, are situated in the midst of its courts and links and command exceedingly pretty views. Its list of members reaches to the number of about two hundred ladies and gentlemen. There is an excellent cricket pitch in front of the club, and although this once supremely popular game has to some extent suffered through the introduction of golf and croquet, some first-rate cricket is often played here. The sunny yet cool climate seems to breed enthusiasm for sports and amusements of all kinds. Bumblepuppy jymkhanas are frequent, when the gentler sex is especially to the fore in every sort of competition, from tilting at the ring to the driving race of geckoes, porcupines and all manner of quaint animals. Dances at the club are frequent, and indoor games with dances interspersed have been introduced. The visitor for a short period has every opportunity of joining in these amusements, and it is this welcome to the stranger that I wish to impress upon those who have not visited Ceylon. "You must come up the wonderful mountain railway into the pure fresh air—away past Kandy, with its sacred Buddhist relics,

NUWARA ELIYA V. COLTS AT THE UNITED CLUB.

NUWARA ELIYA FROM MAHAGASTOTA.

away to the lily garden of Nuwara Eliya, where the scenery is as beautiful as at the Engadine and the air as pure as at St. Moritz. . . . In all my travels I have not met one single individual so far who has not voted enthusiastically for Ceylon as one of the most charming spots on earth." Thus wrote Mr. Clement Scott eight years ago, and since that time the attractions of Nuwara Eliya have greatly increased.

CHAPTER XIX.

HAKGALLA.

WE have already noticed the shallow gap on the mountain heights, which forms the exit from Nuwara Eliya on the Uva side. This gap leads to a lovely gorge, which extends to the foot of the majestic Hakgalla, where the clouds descend in saturating mist during the wet season. This is the most interesting drive in the neighbourhood. For five miles the descent is steep. The precipitous crags have been cut away for the construction of the road, which in its winding course affords grand views of deep wooded ravines, covered with tree ferns in wonderful variety, and teeming with cataracts.

Beneath the rock, which in its form and outline is one of the notable things in Ceylon, nestle the Hakgalla Gardens. While these gardens are no less than 5,400 feet above the sea, this mighty crag towers above them to the height of a further 1,600 feet. Here is a spot famous for picnic breakfasts, usually discussed in an arbour with an unbroken view of the undulating plains of Uva stretching far below.

The Gardens, beautiful in themselves, owe much to their situation, and are the seat of experiments

NATIVE TREE FERNS AT HAKGALLA.

in the acclimatisation of plants from temperate lands outside the tropics and from the tropical heights of other countries. We are surprised at the number of trees and shrubs, and the variety of fruits and flowers that are rarely to be found in a tropical garden. In addition to acclimatisation, the all-important work of extending and improving the various species of indigenous plants is carried on, in order that the natural resources of the country may be utilised to the best advantage. In this place of practical science agricultural theories are translated into actual fact, and provide invaluable material for the enterprise and speculation of the colonist.

Although the main purpose is kept strictly in view, the Gardens are planned with such excellent taste, and the natural features of their situation are so romantic and beautiful, that they form a great attraction to the unscientific spectator. The ornamental creeks and pools; the shrubberies planted with trees of varied foliage; the trickling streams from the mountain tops, with their fringes of native ferns; the flametree blazing above its trunk clad with cream-blossomed creepers; rocky beds covered with maidenhair ferns in the shade of spreading trees with their lovely parasitic growth of orchids; the handsome *Pinus longifolia*, with its fourteen-inch leaves; the hundred kinds of roses; the giant banana; and even the true English oak, as a good omen, keeping in countenance British enterprise in this far-off land—these are a few of the many features of unfailing interest to the casual observer.

In the body of the fernery the native tree ferns (*Alsophila crinita*), for which these Gardens are celebrated, form a striking group. The trunks are mostly eighteen to twenty feet high, and the spreading fronds fifteen to twenty feet across. This species is one of the most stately and graceful of tree ferns, and fine specimens are to be seen in every ravine. The unexpanded fronds are a favourite food of the wild elephant, which inhabits this locality in great numbers. In one respect this fern resembles the cocoanut palm—it grows from the crown, and the lower fronds fall off as the new ones appear above. Until they die off, they hang down the stem of the tree as in the cocoanut, but with this difference, that whereas the frond of the latter comes away entirely, leaving a ring mark upon the trunk, the frond of the tree fern breaks off, leaving the base of the stem on the pithy trunk as a sort of protection.

In addition to the rich botanical feast which the Gardens afford, the student of zoology is well catered for. The curious hoarse cry of the monkeys in their gambols on the trees, where they may be seen leaping from branch to branch; giant worms of cerulean hue, five feet long and an inch thick, are calculated to startle the stranger; black and grey squirrels and creeping things innumerable are to be seen; and many other animals, such as the civet cat, the leopard, the jackal, the deer, the porcupine, the elephant, and the hog, though not often visible, nevertheless inhabit the thick surrounding jungles.

I need only add for the information of visitors to Ceylon that they will find in Mr. W. Nock, the superintendent of these Gardens, a gentleman ever ready to give them a hearty welcome and a botanical feast.

A FIELD OF TREE FERNS NEAR ADAM'S PEAK.

THE EASTERN EXIT FROM NUWARA ELIYA (*see page* 286).

CHAPTER XX.

THE UVA COUNTRY.

WE have referred to the extensive view of undulating plains stretching away to the east from Hakgalla Gardens. This prospect, so different from all we have seen on the western side of the mountain system, is peculiar to the district of Uva. It is a vast mountain ledge about 1,500 feet below Nuwara Eliya, and about six hundred square miles in extent. At various lofty points around Nuwara Eliya it bursts upon the gaze—a splendid panorama of grassy hills surrounded by lofty blue mountains. To pass through any one of the gaps which lead thither is like a sudden transition to a new country. Not only is the spectacle startling, but the climate differs entirely from that of all the other districts. It is drier and usually the air seems more astir. The province of Uva, as marked off by the Government for administrative purposes, includes several divisions which descend into the lowlands; but we shall use the term Uva principally in reference to the highland portion of it. This includes several notable divisions that are cultivated by our own countrymen. One of these, Udapussellawa,* is easily reached from Nuwara Eliya, and we will therefore pay a short visit to this first.

* Udapussellawa is in the Central Province, but is really part of the great mountain ledge popularly known as the Uva country.

If we take the eastern exit from the plains of Nuwara Eliya and leave the Barrack Plains Lake on our right, we shall find five miles of the best road in Ceylon winding up an easy incline to Kandapola, which place is the entrance to the Udapussellawa district. On our way thither we shall pass through some estates which, notwithstanding their great elevation, are famous alike for their yield and the high

UDAPUSSELLAWA.

quality of their tea: Pedro after the famous mountain where it is situated, Lovers' Leap after the legend to which we have already made reference, Portswood, and other estates of the Nuwara Eliya Company are all seen earning their large dividends, the bushes seeming to enjoy the cool atmosphere much more than do the miserable pluckers, who, partially unclad, and by nature suited to withstand extreme heat rather than cold, must in these altitudes suffer great discomfort compared to their fellow-workers at lower and warmer elevations. But no sooner do we pass through the gap into the Uva country than the temperature seems milder. Our view is taken at the very entrance to the district. The belts of gums and grevilleas which seem to divide the estates into fields as hedges do in the old country, indicate the frequent prevalence of high winds, the effects of which, on the tea, they are grown to minimise. We are soon aware that the tea plant has here found a home that suits its requirements. St. John's Estate, through which we are passing, is a picture of luscious hill-grown tea. It has some magnificent bushes, the finest of which measures sixteen feet in diameter. At the twelfth mile the scenery is exquisite, and the rolling downs characteristic of the Uva country begin. We pause here for a moment attracted by a view of one of the largest estates in the district—Delmar. In extent it is upwards of one thousand acres. It serves our purpose of illustration admirably, as we get the whole estate as well as the bungalow, factory, and cooly lines visible from one spot; moreover, it is a good general specimen of a Ceylon Tea Estate, to illustrate which this photograph was introduced into the Handbook of the Paris Exhibition this year. At the twentieth mile of the excellent carriage road which runs through the district tea cultivation practically ends, and rolling downs thence fill the landscape as far as the eye can reach.

Maturatta, ten miles north of Udapussellawa, is one of the most beautiful planting districts in Ceylon, but it is seldom visited by the traveller owing to the absence of any carriage road thither. The only communication is by bridle paths, and along these all the tea from the seven thousand acres under cultivation has to be carried by coolies to the cart road, a distance varying from six to twelve miles. Ten miles of cart road, to connect this district with Udapussellawa road, and thus with Nuwara Eliya, is urgently wanted.

The distant hill in our picture of Delmar is part of the range which divides the district of Udapussellawa from Uva proper. On the hither side we have a distant view of Amherst Estate, which we notice is divided into fields by belts of grevilleas. Cultivation extends over the whole of this (the northern) side of the range, which reaches from Pidurutallagalla for about fourteen miles in the direction of Badulla. It ends abruptly in a steep descent at Beckington Estate, where a grand view of the opposing ranges which enclose the Uva country is obtained. The southern side of the Udapussellawa range is uncultivated and, as we shall presently see, is covered with patana lands intersected with deep belts of forest. Not many years ago the vast stretches of land which we now see covered with tea were magnificent forests. The remains of these are seen at high elevations where the sale of land by the Crown has been discontinued; or in places where difficulties of transport or unsuitability from other causes have checked the planter's enterprise. Large reserves of Crown forests have also been made for purposes of firewood quite irrespective of climatic considerations. These reserves have in many instances proved a boon to the tea enterprise, and will continue to be so until liquid fuel is made quite practicable and economical for use in the factories.

DELMAR, UDAPUSSELLAWA.

T

To the north of Udapussellawa there is a large native district known as Walapane, inhabited by Kandyan Singhalese, and to a considerable extent cultivated by them. It stretches some twenty miles north, as far as the banks of the Mahaweliganga. The traveller who cares for the study of native life may profitably visit the villages of this division, where he will find primitive methods employed both in manufactures and agriculture. The natives here make their own ploughs, yokes, axes, and hardware of various kinds; and their cleverly constructed *elas* or irrigation channels are not without interest to the economist. But we shall find it more convenient to give our attention to such things in passing through the Uva country from Hakgalla to Badulla, whither we now propose to wend our way. For this purpose we return to Nuwara Eliya and again set out in the direction of Hakgalla, prepared, this time, for a two days' drive.

We have already gazed across the arena of the vast amphitheatre, to which this part of Uva has been likened, from the Hakgalla Gardens, and from this elevated position we have received the impression that the thousands of grassy hills which lie at our feet are desolate and devoid of any interest apart from the beauty which their contour lends to the landscape from these heights. That this impression, due to the limited power of human vision, is false we are now about to discover. Closer inspection will reveal countless villages and rivers flowing through extensive gorges whose steep sides are terraced and cultivated by the aid of an irrigation system almost as old as the hills themselves. Form and colour alone fill the eye from the encircling heights; the fair beauty of the glens and the primitive life of the inhabitants are seen only by the enterprising traveller.

One peculiar feature in the distant landscape just now arrests the attention of the visitor: a number of strong white patches are visible upon a couple of smooth and rounded hills. This strange innovation is the camp of the Boer prisoners-of-war. That this fair province should be thus invaded is a matter of regret to some people. Such a circumstance is, however, by no means out of keeping with the traditions of the place, which has been the scene of terrible wars even in the present century. We shall pass through this camp in our peregrinations.

From Hakgalla a good macadamised road reaches right across the Uva *arena* to the beautiful little town of Badulla, which nestles at the foot of Namunacoola, one of the lofty mountains that enclose Uva on the south-east. The distance is about thirty-five miles. Evidence will soon be forthcoming to show that we require two days for the journey. In the first nine miles we drop about two thousand five hundred feet. The gradients, varying from one in ten to one in twenty, are very trying to horseflesh, but we travel in a light Canadian waggon with powerful brake, and at a slow pace there is nothing to detract from the full enjoyment of the scenery, while the bracing atmosphere has a most exhilarating effect on the senses. Save at a few dangerous corners where bullock-carts have occasionally been blown over, the precipitous edge of the road has no terror for the accustomed traveller, although as a first experience it would be alarming enough.

At about the twelfth mile from Nuwara Eliya we

UVA, FROM WILSON'S BUNGALOW, LOOKING TOWARDS UDAPUSSELLAWA.

find a roadside bungalow of considerable pretensions which was built upwards of sixty years ago by Sir John Wilson, commandant of the forces. Since that time it has been restored and used as a rest-house for travellers, but more recently has become a private residence. The situation of this house is romantic and beautiful, and as the surrounding country affords a great variety of sport it was, in its rest-house days, a famous hostelry for hunting parties.

We now realize, as we look back and around, how completely we are surrounded by ranges of lofty mountains. Behind us towers Hakgalla and the Pedro range, continued eastward by Udapussellawa, the southern or uncultivated side of which is now in full view; next towers aloft Narangala with its pilot cone; the south-east is occupied by the grand Namunacoola, reaching nearly seven thousand feet, and the Haputale range; next come Dambaketiya and Totapella to the west, completing the circle.

We are also by this time fully disillusioned about the desolate appearance of the rolling patanas; for deep glens and prosperous villages are now frequently passed as we wind around the conical hills. At one of these villages, called Welimada, we halt for the night. Here we find an excellent rest-house, and every opportunity to make some little study of native life and occupation in the very heart of this unique province. First of all we are attracted by the picturesque character of the village. Everything is opposed to the impressions we received upon Hakgalla. A glance at our picture will verify this. Here is the river flowing under a quaint bridge and between banks which are clad with the richest vegetation, bordering the most fertile gardens and fields. Some of the quaint huts of the village are seen on the left of the picture, embowered in luxuriant foliage. We set out to investigate the methods of cultivation, and are at once struck by the ingenuity displayed in laying out channels for conveying water to the various fields. The precious fertiliser is supplied in abundance from the mountains which we see around us, and the Singhalese husbandman, who from time immemorial has practised the art of irrigation, knows how to secure it by the deflection of river courses, the use of dams, and the manipulation of sluices. He conveys it to gardens and fields at his will, and thus to some extent he can control the periods of cultivation. In another work* I have shown how completely this was done in ancient times, and it is not surprising to find the descendants of a great nation who were unrivalled in their knowledge of the art of irrigation two thousand years ago practising it with some success to-day.

A very interesting account of a Singhalese Ela in this district has been given by Mr. William Hall, of the Public Works Department, who traced the channel of a tunnel watercourse, which skirts the base of Totapella, one of the mountains mentioned above, catches the water of five streams whose natural course would have been towards Dickoya, or Maskeliya, and conveys it by an underground tunnel two hundred and twenty yards long, ten feet high, and forty feet below the surface, to the sunny plains of Uva. "It was my pleasing

---

* "The Ruined Cities of Ceylon," by Henry W. Cave. Sampson Low, Marston & Co., Ltd.

THE VILLAGE OF WELIMADA.

duty," says Mr. Hall, "to trace out this channel and to lead the waters of the five streams in question back into the *Boohoocottoo*, or tunnel.

"The origin and history of this *Boohoo-Ella* may convey an idea of the troublous time which prevailed in Ceylon, from the date of reliable history to the date of its annexation to the British Crown. Here was, for its day, a grand achievement, a water-course eight miles in extent, brought through a tunnel, and dropped into a district against the rules of nature—so to speak—a channel that originally must have irrigated fields ten or twelve miles down the valley of Uva, and yet when first brought to the notice of the then Government Agent, Mr. Bailey (in 1857), there were not three men in the neighbourhood who had heard of it as a work of art. They had a vague idea that the stream (then a very insignificant one) came through a cavern, or *Boohoo*, but nothing more.

"When poor Bailey heard of the existence of this singular tunnel, he clambered up the stream till, after much exertion, he found the water trickling through a tunnel excavated in quartz-gravel; he crawled through this passage over *débris* and rank vegetation, till he emerged upon the opposite side; then he followed up a small channel, and traced it for a mile to a river flowing down from Totapella, and going towards Maskeliya. Beyond this river, no trace of channel or water-course existed—and the problem to be solved seemed to be: Why any man should have gone to the immense trouble to convey the water of such an insignificant stream through a tunnel into Uva, and further, how such an insignificant stream could, even in the course of centuries, have worn so large a water-course as existed *below* the tunnel? In this condition Mr. Bailey left the matter, when he went to the post of Assistant Colonial Secretary, and it was not till five years later that the mystery was solved. It was then discovered that just beyond this first stream, the Ela had been carried away by a bank-slip of immense proportions, and that beyond this slip the channel might be traced for over six miles; and it was discovered that the Ela was constructed to catch the water of five large streams! In the course of further explorations, it was found that five shafts had been sunk, and the tunnel dug from one to the other; and curious to record, though this tunnel had probably been in existence for 200 years, it was not lined or cased with any masonry or other sheathing!"

It has frequently been said that native irrigation is a lost art. As compared with its practice in early times this may be so; but there is a useful remnant of it. We now see how it is possible to carry on the system known as "wet cultivation" upon the hill-sides of the deep glens, and having solved what at first appeared to us a mystery akin to the question of how the milk gets into the cocoanut, our next desire is an acquaintance with the rice-grower and a closer examination of his methods. With this purpose in view we set out for the fields.

The waving corn is in the ripening stage and our attention is soon arrested by mysterious noises that occur in every direction. They are due to an elaborate arrangement for scaring birds which is carried out in the following manner: A crop-watcher's hut is formed with bamboos and plaited cocoanut fronds

THE CROP-WATCHER'S HUT.

as seen in our picture, and from this lines of cord, made from cocoanut fibre, extend in all directions, communicating with ingeniously constructed rattles of an alarmingly discordant nature. Thus the inhabitants of the crop-watcher's hut are enabled effectively to scare both animals and birds who would otherwise rob them of the fruits of their labour. But they do not depend solely upon these

CROP-WATCHING BOWMEN.

devices: this little hut is the temporary dwelling of the whole family of persons who cultivate the fields; they reside in it night and day during the ripening period and each occupant is armed with a bow and stones. The bows are similar to those used with arrows, but they have an additional string and are employed to hurl stones. We try them and our amateur efforts are disappointing—not to say painful; but the natives are expert in their use, seldom failing to hit their mark at considerable range. The enemies of the rice-grower are not limited to birds and small creatures, but include all manner of wild animals whose depredations need the most constant watchfulness.

The subjects of our photographs never previously having seen a camera are at first somewhat scared, but we endeavour through our native attendant to reassure them with some explanation of its use and the purpose to which the pictures will be applied. But it is evident that they can no more understand the *picture box* or its purposes than a child of tender years can comprehend the laws of electric currents. Our interpreter therefore turns to us with the expression, " Sir, these people are wild cats, they cannot understand pictures."

Well! they at least understand rice cultivation, and this is how they carry it on: The classic implement illustrated on page 103 is first introduced and the soddened soil is broken by its iron shoe, which follows the track of the powerful buffalo as he trudges through the mire. Next the terraces are thoroughly waterlogged by means of the low artificial banks or mounds about a foot high with which they are surrounded. Herds of buffaloes are now turned loose into the muddy lakelets where they work the clods left by the plough into a state of slush. The seed is then scattered upon the wet soil, and the buffaloes have an easy time until the harvest. In many places where there is jungle land they are left to roam at large and forage for themselves for a great part of the year, and since in species they are the same as the wild buffalo they often become somewhat dangerous in the temporary freedom which they are permitted to enjoy. Their natural desire is to wallow in mud; so they betake themselves to pools and marshy lands where they can protect their hides from the torment of numberless insects.

We have seen the occupation of the husbandman while the corn is ripening. His task is rendered the less arduous inasmuch as the corn grows thickly and itself keeps down weeds. In the early part of the growth he has constantly to regulate the water supply; for the soil is not allowed to dry until the grain begins to ripen, and then only gradually. Rice grows a tall and stiff straw as will be seen in our picture, the average height being four feet. Reaping is done with the sickle just as it used to be in Europe; and the subsequent operations are no less primitive. After the sun has dried the sheaves they are gathered up and placed in heaps. The buffaloes are then requisitioned again for the purpose of treading the grain off the ears. This would seem a less laborious task for them than the earlier processes of the culture, but, heedless of the muzzle as they are, they doubtless prefer to wallow in mud rather than tread upon clean straw.

Before the husk has been removed rice is generally called paddy, and in this form it is used for the food of horses and other animals. It is a coarse grain something like barley without the beard; the outer shell conceals the bran beneath which is the pure grain of rice. The husks are removed by simple pounding in a mortar of hard wood and the chaff is separated by the manipulation of sieves and trays with the help of the wind.

Our interest in these agricultural proceedings is unfortunately liable to a most objectionable kind of interference, which may utterly destroy the serenity of mind induced by the idyllic charm of our surroundings, and, moreover, may be the cause of both thoughts and expressions that nobody wishes to have or to use. If we carefully choose the time of our visit to the fields when the sun has dried the surfaces of the mounds that border the terraces, and avoid paths which are moist from their approximation to the water-courses we may escape the evil. But if we wander indiscriminately, thousands of eyes will be turned upon us from creatures having five pairs each: and they undoubtedly want our blood. Above all things it behoves the amateur photographer to be careful where he stands with his head covered by a dark cloth; for, judging from my own experience, this is the favourite opportunity of the terrestrial ten-eyed leech of the Ceylon highlands. Our experience of these mysterious pests exactly accords with Sir Emerson Tennent's description: "In size they are about an inch in length, and as fine as a common knitting needle; but capable of distension till they equal a quill in thickness, and attain a length of nearly two inches. Their structure is so flexible that they can insinuate themselves through the meshes of the finest stocking, not only seizing on the feet and ankles, but ascending to the back and throat and fastening on the tenderest parts of the body. In moving they have the power of planting one extremity on the earth and raising the other perpendicularly to watch for their victim. Such is their vigilance and instinct, that on the approach of a passer-by to a spot which they infest, they may be seen amongst the grass and fallen leaves on the edge of a native path, poised erect and preparing for their attack on man and horse. On descrying their prey they advance rapidly by semicircular strides, fixing one end firmly and arching the other forwards, till by successive advances they can lay hold of the traveller's foot, when they disengage themselves from the ground and ascend his dress in search of an aperture to enter. Their size is so insignificant, and the wound they make is so skilfully punctured, that both are generally imperceptible, and the first intimation of their onslaught is the trickling of blood or the chill feeling of the leech."

The visitor need not, however, be alarmed by this story, for as a rule he does not tread the wet grass where the pest is found; and if he should have occasion to do so there are means of preventing attacks, such as leech gaiters. The natives keep them off by smearing the legs with oil. They rarely appear at the lowest, nor yet at the highest altitudes; but parts of Uva have always been infested by them during rainy weather. Indeed it is on record that some of the troops actually perished from their attacks during the wars of the early part of the century, to which we shall presently make reference. "One circumstance regarding these land leeches," says Tennent, "is remarkable and unexplained; they are helpless without moisture, and in the hills where they abound at other times, they entirely disappear during long droughts; yet reappear instantaneously on the very first fall of rain; and in spots previously parched, where not one was visible an hour before. A single shower is sufficient to reproduce them in thousands, lurking beneath the decaying leaves. Whence do they reappear? Do they, too, take a summer sleep like the reptiles, molluscs, and tank fishes, or may they be, like the *Rotifera*, dried up and preserved for an indefinite period, resuming their vital activity on the mere recurrence of moisture?"

Upon our return from the fields we pass through the village bazaar where every product of the district is displayed in open stalls. Here, too, we find the enterprising and ubiquitous moorman, whose wares comprise necessities and luxuries from the coast towns. We are somewhat astonished at the variety of grain, fruit and vegetables to be found in this market, which presents a great contrast to the squalid and poverty-stricken appearance of the village shops in the north-central province. We learn, however, that Welimada is prosperous above the average even of the Uva villages, a circumstance due to its position on the great turnpike from Kandy to Badulla; for near this village many bridle paths and minor roads from the estates upon the distant hills converge. One of these, from Udapussellawa, enters the village by the quaint roofed-bridge which will be noticed in our photograph on page 297. The purpose of the thatched roofing, we are told, is to protect the timber of the bridge from sun and rain, and thus prolong its life.

As the sun sinks below the crest of the western range dusky maidens in continuous procession are seen carrying their *water-chatties* to the spring; for it is time to cook the evening meal of rice and curry, and fresh water is being fetched for this purpose. Next the culinary art is displayed before our curious eyes. With a few earthenware bowls and the mud

THE VILLAGE BAZAAR OF WELIMADA.

floor to do duty for both table and stove, Nonahamy can cook the most savoury viands. They may not be inviting to the English palate, but they are cleverly cooked and served; and notwithstanding the squalid appearance of the hut the food thus produced is clean and wholesome. The cultivated plots around the huts supply the vegetable portion,

NONAHAMY PRACTISING THE CULINARY ART.

which consists chiefly of gourds, brinjals, cucumbers, and bandakai.

The simple pastoral life in these highland glens reminds us of our youthful studies in ancient Jewish history; for much that the Old Testament describes may be seen here to-day, where customs and modes of life have remained unchanged for thousands of years.

For a short period during the days of successful coffee planting Welimada was in danger of innovations; but since the advent of tea other roads and railways have diverted the traffic from the estates cultivated by the British, and the village has retained its comparative isolation. After the hurry and bustle of Europe it is refreshing for the traveller to come across such primitive communities. There is no wealth, nor does it appear even to have been sought; but there is no want. One thing is made clear to us—the fact that people can be contented and happy without many possessions. If happiness is, as Aristotle thought, the end of all our actions, such consummation is easier of attainment by the Uva villager than the European.

But Uva has had its periods of trouble—even bloodshed and devastation. There are many unoccupied military posts and deserted forts scattered about the province, and it is curious that, although the strife of battle is never again likely to disturb the Singhalese inhabitants, martial law is once more in force within the province, owing to the presence of the Boer prisoners-of-war. The previous occasion, however, when British troops found the task of subduing a rising in Uva not very dissimilar or less difficult, *mutatis mutandis*, than the present trouble in South Africa, is more within our province to discuss. As we proceed from Welimada to Badulla we observe what a difficult fighting country we are in. The rounded hills and deep gorges do not look so insignificant as they did from the heights around Nuwara Eliya, and we find the country around Attampitiya particularly steep and rugged—not unlike some parts of the Transvaal country.

Uva, owing to its situation and the difficulty of communication with Kandy, was in earlier times

GORGE NEAR ATTAMPITIYA.

governed by very powerful chiefs, and was even regarded at one time as an independent state.

The Portuguese were the first Europeans to invade it, but the expedition was very disastrous to them. Tennent gives a succinct account of it: "Don Constantine de Sa, stung by sarcastic despatches from the Viceroy of Goa, which insinuated inactivity and indifference to the interests of Portugal, was induced by delusive representations from the chief of the high country to concentrate all his forces for an expedition against Uva, where he was falsely assured that the population were prepared to join his standard against their native dynasty. In August A.D. 1630 he advanced with fifteen hundred Europeans, about the same number of half-castes, and eight or ten thousand low-country Sinhalese, and was allowed without resistance to enter by the mountain passes and penetrate to the city of Badulla, which he plundered and burned. But on his return his Sinhalese troops, at a point previously arranged with the Kandyans, deserted in a body to the enemy, and the Portuguese, thus caught in the toils, were mercilessly slaughtered, and the head of their commander carried on a drum and presented to Raja Singha, the son of the Emperor, who was bathing in a neighbouring brook."

The people of Uva had never been conquered by the foreigner, and it is not surprising that they were somewhat disturbed by the changes brought about in their country by the British occupation. The new government had been very kind and indulgent towards them, and had, moreover, got rid of a tyrant king under whom they had suffered. Nevertheless they attempted the expulsion of their benefactors. Dr. Davy, who was an eye-witness of the troublous time, says: "The natives never met us boldly in the field: they had recourse to stratagem of every kind, and took every possible advantage of the difficult nature of their country and of their minute knowledge of the ground. They would waylay our parties and fire on them from inaccessible heights, or from the ambush of an impenetrable jungle; they would line the paths through which we had to march with snares of different kinds—such as spring guns and spring bows, deep pits lightly covered over, and armed with thorns, spikes, etc., and in every instance that an opportunity offered they showed no mercy and gave no quarter. There were certain redeeming circumstances occasionally exhibited on which one might dwell with pleasure: traits of heroism amongst our men, and of undaunted courage that has never been exceeded; and traits of parental attachment amongst the natives, of cool resignation to their fate, that have seldom been surpassed."

This guerilla war with the English in 1817–18 was kept up for about a year, during which time we lost about one thousand men and the Singhalese about ten thousand. The British had undertaken an almost impossible task, and "for many months," says Tennent, "discomfiture seemed imminent and so universal was the conspiracy of the inhabitants that not a Kandyan leader of any consequence was taken, and not a district was either pacified or subdued. So great was the apprehension of the Government, and such the horrors of the species of warfare in which they were involved, that the expediency had already been discussed of abandoning the contest and

A KANDYAN CHIEF.

withdrawing the British forces to the coast, when towards the close of 1818, the Kandyans, harassed by the destruction of their villages and cattle, rendered destitute by the devastation of their country, and disheartened by the loss of upwards of ten thousand persons, either fallen in the field or destroyed by famine and fever, began to throw out signals of submission. The rebellious chiefs were captured; the pretender fled; the great palladium, 'the sacred tooth' of Buddha, which had been stolen and paraded to arouse the fanatical enthusiasm of the people, was recovered and restored to its depository in Kandy; and before the close of the year the whole country returned to tranquillity and order. The rebellion of 1817 was the last great occasion on which the English forces were arrayed in hostility against the natives of any portion of Ceylon."

No one is now alive who saw the devastation which took place in Uva in that terrible year: its fields lying waste, its population almost destroyed, its cattle so many skeleton carcases, and its villages in ruins. It has recovered from the terrible scourge, and a new generation has grown up without the prejudices of their forefathers—prejudices which we must admit were just, and deserved more consideration than they sometimes received from the invader. We have learned better methods of gaining the confidence and goodwill of oriental people since the days of the Uva rebellion; and the causes which led to that and other similar troubles now seem to us melancholy reading. Dr. Davy was a shrewd observer, and the following words from his account may be taken as correctly describing the real cause of disaffection: "There was no sympathy between us and them; no one circumstance to draw or bring us together, and innumerable ones of a repulsive nature. The chiefs though less controlled than under the King, and exercising more power in their districts than they ever before ventured to exert, were far from satisfied. Before, no one but the King was above them; now, they were inferior to every civilian in our service—to every officer in our army. Though officially treated with respect, it was only officially; a common soldier passed a proud Kandyan chief with as little attention as he would a fellow of the lowest caste. Thus they considered themselves degraded and shorn of their splendour.

The people in general had similar feelings on this score; at least, the respectable and most considerable portion of the population, viz., the Goewanse part. Ignorant of their distinctions, high caste and low caste were treated alike by most Englishmen who came in contact with them, and undesignedly and unknowingly we offended and provoked them when we least intended it; and particularly in our mode of entering their temples, and in our manner of treating their priests, who require respect amounting almost to adoration; accustomed to the presence of a King in their capital, to the splendour of his court, and to the complicated arrangements connected with it, they could ill relish the sudden and total abolition of the whole system. The King of Great Britain was to them merely a name; they had no notion of a King ruling over them at a distance of thousands of miles; they had no notion of delegated authority; they wanted a King whom they could see, and before whom they could prostrate and obtain summary justice. These are only a few of the leading

BADULLA AT THE FOOT OF NAMUNACOOLA.

circumstances which tended to render the natives averse to us and our government, and anxious to attempt to throw it off."

The Singhalese are now very contented, and recognise the advantages of forming part of the British Empire. They prefer Englishmen in places of authority, and even consider it a grievance if they have not got them.

The capital of the province of Uva is Badulla, a

BADULLA: AVENUE OF INGA SAMAN TREES.

very picturesque little town situated in a charming valley at the foot of the noble mountain Namunacoola. In approaching it we have descended from an elevation of four thousand to about two thousand feet, and consequently we find the climate warmer. This lower elevation favours tropical verdure and we see in Badulla the beautiful trees and palms that we miss in the Uva *arena*. Upon entering the town the traveller is impressed by the architectural merit and substantial form of the public buildings, the well-kept appearance of the place, and the fine trees by which the broad roads are everywhere shaded. A river, whose banks are clothed with beautiful vegetation, almost encircles the town and supplies the *elas* which irrigate vast stretches of paddy fields. After pursuing a course which contributes greatly to agricultural facilities as well as picturesqueness the

THE BADULLA HOSPITAL.

waters flow through a narrow gorge and over a precipitous rock forming the exquisite Dunhinda Falls.

Upon entering the town the judge's bungalow will be first noticed on a knoll to the right, and as we proceed the hospital, which we illustrate, comes into view on the left. Next we pass the market, which is an ornamental as well as very useful institution. Here we notice a plentiful supply of fine fruit,

THE DISTRICT COURT, BADULLA.

suggesting at once that we are in a fruit-growing district. Indeed we soon find this to be the case; for nowhere do we get better pine-apples and oranges than are spread before us in abundance at the rest-house. The pine-apples, eighteen inches in circumference and of unequalled flavour, will be remembered by the traveller when other details of his visit have long faded from his mind. From the market extends one of the most beautiful avenues of Inga Saman, or

THE MARKET, BADULLA.

rain trees, that can be found anywhere. It will be remembered that we examined the peculiarities of this tree at Matale (see page 96).

On the right of the avenue is an extensive grassy bank over which a grand view of Namunacoola can be seen, his lofty brow frequently enshrouded in mist, as in our picture on page 321. On the left of the avenue we notice several pretentious buildings, including the District Court, the Police Barracks, and the Kachcheri, or seat of provincial government. The last named building is on the site of the old star Fort, the earthworks of which remain. In earlier times the palace of the Prince of Uva is said to have stood there.

The province is administered by the Government Agent and his staff from the Kachcheri. The area is 3,725 square miles, and the population about 160,000 Singhalese. For convenience of administration it is formed into seven divisions, each being placed under the care of a native officer called the Ratémahatmaya, who is responsible to the Government Agent and acts under his instructions. There are subdivisions called Kòrales with their subordinate officers; and the villages each have a headman who is made responsible for orderly behaviour. The village communities are subject to rules framed for them by the Government Agent, and the Ratémahatmayas, as Presidents of Village Councils, try cases for breaches of the regulations. All cases which the village rules do not cover are brought before the District Court or one of the minor courts of the capital.

There is an estate population of immigrant Tamils to the number of about 35,000. These are mostly employed on the estates of the British planters which cover the mountains of the Madulsima, Monaragala, and Haputale ranges. These estates, about two hundred in number, have a lion's share in the general prosperity of the province, and it is to them that Badulla owes its development from an insignificant village to a prosperous and beautiful town.

From the present our thoughts and enquiries are

FOUR CROSS ROADS IN THE TOWN OF BADULLA.

turned towards the past by various monuments that we come across. At a corner of the four cross roads visible in our photograph on page 329, is an unpretentious little English Church embowered in foliage of great beauty and variety. The following simple inscription is upon one of its walls :—

A.D. 1845.

THIS CHURCH WAS ERECTED TO THE HONOUR OF GOD,

IN MEMORY OF

THOMAS WILLIAM ROGERS,

MAJOR OF THE CEYLON RIFLE REGIMENT,
ASSISTANT GOVERNMENT AGENT AND DISTRICT JUDGE
OF BADULLA,

BY

ALL CLASSES OF HIS PEOPLE, FRIENDS,
AND ADMIRERS.
HE WAS KILLED BY LIGHTNING AT HAPUTALE,
JUNE 7TH, 1845.

AGED 41.

"IN THE MIDST OF LIFE WE ARE IN DEATH."

Major Rogers held at one and the same time every office of the Government at Badulla. He was Commandant of the Forces, Revenue Administrator, District Judge, and Officer of Public Works. In every branch he was an indefatigable worker, and the greatest sportsman withal that Ceylon has ever seen. In the latter capacity his memory is most popularly perpetuated; but his greatest monuments are the splendid roads which he traced and constructed, including that upon which we have travelled from Nuwara Eliya. His other services to the colony were performed in an equally efficient manner, and at his death it was found that no less than four officers were needed to perform his work; and even then the results were less satisfactory than when all departments were administered by him alone.

When Major Rogers was appointed to Badulla in 1834 the province had scarcely recovered from the devastation of the war of 1818, and, owing to the sparse population, the most destructive wild animals had almost taken possession of the land. Elephants, in particular, roamed in great herds and destroyed the crops of the fields and gardens to such an extent that the natives were greatly discouraged in their agricultural pursuits, and gladly welcomed any sportsman who assisted in reducing their number. Major Rogers made personal warfare against these destroying herds, and in ten years no less than fifteen hundred elephants fell to his rifle. He was an unerring shot, and, although he did such immense slaughter, a wounded elephant seldom got away to die a slow and torturing death in the jungle. Although tusked elephants were always rather scarce in Ceylon they were less so in Rogers' time than now, as we gather from the following notes of Dr. Hoffmeister, who, with Prince Waldemar, visited Rogers in the forties: "His whole house was filled with ivory, for among the hosts of the slain more than sixty were tusked elephants (sixty out of about 1,400). At each door of his verandah stand huge tusks, while in his dining-room every corner is adorned with similar trophies. . . .

"Most fearful adventures indeed has he gone through. On one occasion an infuriated elephant so trampled and crushed him with its feet and trunk, that it was only the depth of the hole into which the latter cast him, that was the means of saving his life. Several of his ribs on the right side were broken by this stamping, which is the usual mode in which an elephant despatches his enemy; his right arm was also broken in three places, and the shoulder dislocated besides. He has seen two of his fellow-sportsmen by similar treatment perish before his eyes; he himself, of iron constitution, has escaped with his life, and a fearful revenge indeed has he taken for his defeat in that memorable adventure."

At length this man of genius and intrepidity, who seemed to have enjoyed a charmed life, since the most infuriated of the brute creation failed in their encounters with him, was stricken by a fatal flash of lightning. He had taken shelter in a rest-house at Haputale pass and was standing under the porch, looking for the abatement of the storm, when a flash, attracted, it was absurdly said, by his military spurs, instantly killed him. His body was removed to Nuwara Eliya and interred in a little cemetery which is situated on a knoll between the present post office and the golf pavilion. There stands the tomb of the talented Major Rogers, who rendered such signal service to the colony, desolate, untended and itself fractured by the same "fire from heaven" that caused his death.

I do not know that blame is attached to anyone for this; but I do know that the circumstance appears shocking to many a visitor who, having read of the exploits and achievements of Major Rogers, visits the solitary tomb. The site of the little disused cemetery is prominent in the landscape, and if a fitting monument to the gallant Major Rogers were now to be erected there, it would be an ornament to Nuwara Eliya as he was an ornament to the service.

Another memorial of very pathetic interest is to be seen in the old cemetery at Badulla, and of this

TOMB OF MRS. WILSON.

we give an illustration. It will be noticed that a Bo-tree, *Ficus Religiosa*, has here almost completely enfolded a tomb, holding it firmly and securely in its embrace. Not a stone can be removed without cutting the tree. Even the inscribed tablet at the end of the tomb is partially embedded; but the tree in this part is kept trimmed so that the inscription may be seen. This tree is the species of fig which is worshipped and held in great veneration by the Buddhists.

The letters in our illustration, on the opposite page, being too small to be easily read we give below a copy of the inscription.

The death of this lady occurred a very short time before the rebellion in which her husband was so soon to fall, the first European victim, shot

SACRED TO THE MEMORY OF

SOPHIA WILSON,

ONLY DAUGHTER OF THE LATE

EDMOND BATTERSBEE, ESQ.,

OF

STRATFORD UPON AVON, WARWICKSHIRE,

WIFE OF

SYLVESTER DOUGLAS WILSON, ESQ.,

ASSISTANT RESIDENT AND AGENT OF THE BRITISH GOVERNMENT IN THE PROVINCE OF OUWA

SHE DEPARTED THIS LIFE
AT BADULLA, AFTER A FEW DAYS' ILLNESS,

ON THE MORNING OF 24TH MAY, 1817.

AGED 24 YEARS.

by an arrow under the following circumstances: Mr. Wilson set out with a guard of about forty troops to investigate causes of disaffection and lawlessness. They soon found that their number was insufficient for the purpose, and were about to return to Badulla when an armed party appeared on the opposite bank of the river and demanded a conference. Mr. Wilson, with intrepidity, advanced to them, but, when within a few yards, a volley of arrows was treacherously discharged at him, and Mr. Wilson and one of his Lascoreens fell. The other ran back and informed Lieutenant Newman, who advanced with 12 men, and was beckoned by the Kandyans to approach. They, however, kept a menacing attitude, and he judged it expedient to fire upon them, when they fled into the jungle; and as he advanced, he met the Lascoreen who had fallen coming towards him with two bad arrow wounds. He pointed out the fatal spot

BADULLA REST-HOUSE.

where Mr. Wilson fell; but, after an ineffectual search for his body till it was dark, it was concluded the Kandyans had carried it off. This was one of the first treacherous acts in the rebellion to which we have referred.

We must now return to our general description of the town. Quite near to the Kachcheri stands the comfortable rest-house with a vista stretching down a fine boulevard in the direction of the

Hospital. It is more than an ordinary rest-house both in its capacity and its cuisine, and might be regarded as a comfortable little hotel. Beyond this is an ornamental fountain on the left, the quarters of the Provincial Engineer on the right, and beyond them standing in extensive grounds is the Residency, the official house of the Government Agent of the province. The Town Hall, which serves as a library and reading-room as well

A BADULLA LANE.

as a place for public meetings, is one of the best institutions of the town, and is situated near the Residency.

There is one more feature of the town which is a growing and important one—the botanic gardens. The climate is so perfectly suited for experimental horticulture that it was thought advisable some ten years ago to establish a branch of Peradeniya here. How successful this departure has been is evident to anyone who visits the gardens. They are already full of marvels, and form a great attraction to both residents and visitors.

Adjoining the gardens is the race-course where the "Merrie men of Uva" assemble annually for the Uva Autumn Meet. We have already referred to the facilities which almost every planting district offers for sport; few, however, can boast of a more picturesque race-course than Badulla. Our photograph unfortunately portrays only the bare course, and it is left to the imagination of the reader to fill in the motley crowd which enlivens the pretty landscape on the occasions of "the meet." The ladies flock thither arrayed in the latest "creations" of Europe which they display upon the lawn and stand, while thousands of natives in Eastern holiday attire form picturesque groups on the banks of the lake and the greensward enclosed by the course.

There is in most Eastern towns an appearance of squalor and filth which the Briton who has not been out of his native land can hardly realise; but Badulla is a proof that there are exceptions. Perhaps the situation of the town, with the Baduluoya sweeping almost completely round it, the sloping streets, and the mild and moist climate which causes the vegetation to absorb noxious matter, may contribute to the wholesome appearance; but to these influences must doubtless be added some quality possessed by the inhabitants which is not universal amongst townspeople in Ceylon. Our lasting impressions of Badulla will be its well-tended buildings and streets and the beautiful trees by which they are shaded; its luxuriant fruit gardens in the valley of the Baduluoya; its pretty race-course and the lovely

BADULLA RACE-COURSE AND LAKE.

DEMODERA TEA FACTORY

pictures of the whole town with its deep borders of bright green paddy fields as seen from the hills that surround it.

We shall now ascend to Bandarawela which lies under the Haputale range on the south of the Uva *arena* and two thousand feet above Badulla. The journey is interesting mainly on account of the flourishing tea and coffee estates through which we pass, and their beautiful situations. For the first four or five miles we pass through a rich valley of rice fields which extends almost to the source of the Baduluoya; and then, as we approach the grand Namunacoola, the famous estate of Spring Valley comes into view. This property possesses in the very highest degree the qualities of picturesqueness and richness of soil combined, notwithstanding that its rocky hillsides rise upwards of two thousand feet from the bottom to the top of the estate. We are told that so steep are some of its declivities that coolies have to be tied to tree stems while doing the work of plucking. The property does not, however, entirely consist of such appalling steeps, but has its rich hollows and gentle slopes in abundance. We learn that the term Spring Valley as originally applied to one estate now embraces a large group to the extent of 2,250 acres, nearly all of which are now planted with tea.

Adjoining this is another large group called Demodera, and as we pass through it we are attracted by the appearance of its fine new tea factory. We have previously referred to the importance of the site in building a factory and the desirability of obtaining water power if possible. Here a site perfect in this respect has been obtained, and we see the water conducted to the turbines from the hills, and the waste flowing onwards to the river.

Upon arrival at Bandarawela the effects of the bracing air which we noticed at Wilson's Bungalow are again apparent, and we look around in surprise at the desolate appearance of a place that possesses so fine a climate, and is moreover the terminus of the mountain railway. Three or four bungalows and a very nice hotel comprise the entire European portion of the place. As we sit beneath the shade of the orange trees in the hotel garden and see the great masses of dense vapour rolling over Nuwara Eliya and the western ranges, and think of the drenching rain that is descending over there, we wonder that so few people find their way into Uva during the rains. Perhaps the reason may be found in the fact that Bandarawela, the only place where hotel accommodation can be found, is practically without water supply, and is also devoid of all attraction in the way of amusements. It has an unrivalled climate; but climate is not all that is needful to attract visitors, and it is to be hoped that the Government Agent of the Province will at least endeavour to obtain an adequate water supply from the Haputale range before long.

Diyatalawa, now famous as the camp of the Boer prisoners-of-war, is visible from the Bandarawela hotel grounds, at a distance of about two miles as the crow flies. The way there, however, is not so easy as it looks, and the pedestrian will find the patana paths very steep and rough. The railway line provides the better route even for foot passengers, although it requires a strong nerve to cross the bridges over ravines sixty to upwards of one hundred

DIYATALAWA, FROM THE CAMP OF THE BOER PRISONERS-OF-WAR.

feet deep; the crossing being effected upon narrow plates of steel which spring under the foot, while the steep abyss is disclosed by wide apertures, and the hand rail at the side is not continuous. Our picture (p. 343) was obtained from this railway and very near to the Camp. It is intended to convey a general idea of the features of the country, around the camp of the Boer prisoners-of-war. It will be admitted that we have been sufficiently considerate to find them a location possessing many of the characteristics of their own country. They are placed upon the *veldt*, guarded from *kopjes*, and surrounded by mountains as rugged and full of cover as their own. Only one-tenth of the camp buildings had been erected when our photographs were taken in June; but there are now upwards of sixty huts of corrugated iron, well finished with windows and floors and supplied with inhabitants. The appearance of the camp is very similar to that of Ladysmith, which was known as the *Tin Town.*

It is not within our province to discuss the policy which has introduced this unique feature into the landscape, beneath the Haputale range; but it will doubtless seem to many readers that there are worse misfortunes than being a prisoner-of-war upon the beautiful downs of Uva. That this view is a correct one, and that the life is the very antithesis of the hardships of campaigning, we gather from the prisoners-of-war themselves. Upon arrival in Ceylon they were at once entranced by its beauty and thoroughly enjoyed the railway journey into the hills. Upon arrival in camp they were still further surprised at the excellence of the arrangements for their comfort, the fine climate, and the beauty of their surroundings. They have no desire to escape from such a place and such treatment as their captors mete out to them. Upon being questioned on this point one of them replied that he would like to live there a hundred years, the officers were most kind, the food and lodging excellent, and the time was allowed to be spent in smoking, reading, cricket, football, quoits, and concerts.

But however happy the ex-warriors of the Transvaal may be upon the downs of Uva, it is to be hoped that peace will soon remove the necessity of the entertainment.

Haputale lies upon the hills that overlook Diyatalawa and should be visited by the traveller, if only for the lovely glimpse of the low country to be obtained, either from the Haldamulla pass, or the ridge that leads to the Lipton group of estates at Koslande. Perhaps the best view may be obtained from a knoll on Pitaratmalie. Here a grand stretch of lowland country may be seen thickly wooded, but diversified with rocky hills that rise very abruptly from the flat land. There is usually considerable haze over these lowlands; but even this is beautiful and lends a lovely blue tint to the whole scene.

From Haputale the railway rises amidst a multitude of broken cliffs and rocky ravines, and through innumerable short tunnels, until it almost climbs to the summit of the highest western range; but before reaching the crest it pierces the rock and suddenly takes us out of sunny Uva into the storms and mists of the west. Nowhere is the curious phenomenon of sudden change of climate, which we described on page 216 so startling as here. The

THE CAMP OF THE BOER PRISONERS-OF-WAR.

prevailing weather on the western end of the tunnel during the south-west monsoon is wet, misty and cold, while on the eastern side, not many yards distant, the whole plains are ablaze with sunshine and the air is crisp and dry. It is even possible to stand on the hill above the summit tunnel with one cheek exposed to pouring torrents of rain and the other to bracing air and sunshine. From summit tunnel the railway gradually descends into the Dimbula district until it reaches Nanu Oya, at which station we alighted for Nuwara Eliya.

THE BAND OF THE HIGHLANDERS.

CHAPTER XXI.

THE KELANI VALLEY.

FROM the foregoing descriptions of the varied and pleasant climates of the highlands of Ceylon it might naturally be supposed that the British colonist would hesitate to settle down to any agricultural pursuit in the heated lowlands; but that this is not so is abundantly proved by the rapid development of tea cultivation in the Kelani Valley, one of the most beautiful, albeit intensely tropical, parts of Ceylon. This district is, moreover, no less interesting from its historical associations than its varied and romantic scenery. It lies on the old route to Kandy, and its principal villages, Avisawela and Ruanwella, were strongholds of the Kandyan Kings, where they met and opposed European forces in many a bloody strife. Some knowledge of the real events which have occurred along this ancient route to the highland capital lends a vivid interest to well nigh every picturesque spot. We have not space to recount the heroic deeds, fierce battles, acts of Oriental treachery and barbarity, and the exciting and adventurous experiences, both of the Portuguese and the British in their several conflicts with the

Kandyan Kings; but we may briefly notice by way of contrast with the present condition of the Kelani Valley what sort of place it was when the British soldier marched through it a century ago. Roughly cut jungle paths, uneven and swampy, here and there impassable for wheeled traffic, and intersected at frequent intervals by wide and rapid streams; no bridges of any kind, and many an artfully contrived *cul de sac*—these were some of the embarrassments experienced by the invader.

The fact of the district being subject to violent thunderstorms, which were immediately followed by the rapid rise and overflow of the rivers, rendered camping a matter of the most serious difficulty; moreover, the jungle was so infested with leeches, that it was often impossible to find any spot secure from their molestation. Even after the greatest precautions had been taken, the soldiers sometimes presented an appearance absolutely shocking, covered as they were with blood, and many of them having upwards of a hundred leeches adhering to their bodies at one time. Men would suppose only that they were in a profuse perspiration, but, upon removing their garments, they would find themselves literally covered with these voracious creatures, and bleeding from head to foot.

Inconveniences such as these, added to the great heat, and the necessity of patching up the roads through ravines and defiles, might well be supposed to distract the soldier's attention from those scenes, the natural beauty of which delights the traveller of the present day, enjoying as he does, the advantages of splendid roads, good rest-houses, and every comfort; but so romantic and beautiful is the landscape in every direction, that some of the military officers who experienced all the trials and embarrassments which we have mentioned, described it in their journals in terms of such glowing enthusiasm that it is evident their privations did not prevent them from being enchanted by the singular beauty of the country disclosed to them by their undaunted efforts.

No such spirit of adventure is required to explore the wilds of the Kelani Valley in the present day. The same fascinating landscape of undulating lowlands and lovely river views is there, but the modern traveller finds, not only excellent roads, but always a courteous, gentle, and contented population. I know of no other district in which Singhalese rural life is more full of interest. Even a visit to Hanwella is well repaid, although it necessitates a journey of twenty-one miles from Colombo. The primitive methods of the natives in the manufacture of the quaintest pottery, their curious system of agriculture, and the peculiar phases of their social life, are no less interesting than the beautiful country in which they live.

The elegant Areca-nut Palms form one of the most noticeable features of the district. They adorn the jungle on all sides. A pleasing effect is produced by the beautiful delicate stem, with its rich feathery crest, upon the surrounding foliage. The graceful bamboos, the huge waving fronds of the plantain, the shapely mango, covered with the bell-shaped blossoms of the Thunbergia creeper, all seem to form a setting in which the elegant Areca displays its beauties to the greatest possible advantage.

The quality of picturesqueness, however, is not

A ROADSIDE SCENE IN THE KELANI VALLEY.

X

THE JAK TREE.

the only virtue of this tree. It is very prolific in the production of nuts, which grow in clusters from the stem just beneath the crest of the palm. Previous to the development of the nuts the tree flowers, and diffuses a delightful fragrance all around. In size and appearance the nuts are not unlike the nutmeg, and are similarly enclosed in a husk. What becomes of them is easy to realise when it is considered that every man, woman, and child is addicted to the habit of betel chewing, and that the areca-nut forms part of the compound used for this purpose; added to this, there is an export trade in areca-nuts to the amount of about £75,000 per annum.

Another tree attracts the notice of every traveller by its stupendous growth and gigantic fruit—the Jak. It not only grows the largest of all edible fruits, but it bears it in prodigious quantity and in a very peculiar manner. It throws huge pods from the trunk and the larger branches, and suspends them by a thick short stalk. I have counted as many as eighty of these huge fruits upon one tree, some of them weighing as much as forty to fifty pounds. They are pale green in colour, with a granulated surface. Inside the rough skin is a soft yellow substance, and embedded in this are some kernels about the size of a walnut. This fruit often forms an ingredient in the native curries, but its flavour is not liked by Europeans. Elephants, however, are very fond of it, and its great size would seem to make it an appropriate form of food for these huge beasts. After the elephant in our picture on page 367 had been photographed, he was rewarded with a feast of this fruit, which grew plentifully on the trees upon the banks of the river,

One circumstance should make this district a very popular resort for travellers, who too frequently see only the towns, and leave Ceylon without an idea of pure Singhalese life, or of the beauty of the tropical scenery of the low-country valleys. I refer to the excellent rest-houses, which are stationed at convenient intervals, and which provide suitable food and

THE RIVER KELANI, FROM KADUWELLA REST-HOUSE.

accommodation to the visitor. I cannot say quite so much in favour of the Coach service, although it is interesting in its way, and at any rate provides some excitement, pleasant enough for those who are not of a nervous disposition, albeit somewhat uninviting to the timid. Let me describe the methods peculiar to the Ceylon Coach.

When a horse's bolting propensities are found to be incurable, when his proneness to kick the tiles out of his stable roof has become a nuisance and expense, when he has completely smashed his owner's carriage, and knocked down the columns of his portico, and, by way of varying his escapades, has tossed his rider over a cinnamon bush, and has escaped from the saddle without breaking the girths, with the additional trifle of driving his hoofs into the lungs of the muttu, or horse-keeper, he is there-

THE ROYAL MAIL COACH

upon considered to have earned his promotion to the service of Her Majesty's Royal Mail Coach.

The Royal Mail Coach itself is not subject to damage, and even if the passengers are, the clever boys, whose business it is to persuade the gentle brutes to draw the coach, generally manage to contrive that no one gets hurt.

The entertainment provided for the passengers is, therefore, somewhat after the following fashion: A start is made from the General Post Office in

Colombo with a coach something after the style of a huge waggonette, roughly constructed, but of a solid character, and surmounted by a large canopy, which serves as a protection from the sun, and is supported by iron rods affixed to the sides of the vehicle.

To this machine, for the first stage of the journey, a pair of horses of only third-rate vicious propensity are attached by means of scanty and unsafe-looking

VILLAGERS WATCHING THE ROYAL MAIL PASS.

odd pieces of leather and iron links, which in some remote past may have done duty as good harness, but which now bear little resemblance to that commodity.

It would not do to start from the capital with horses of first-class coaching characteristics, because the way lies for three miles through the thickly populated suburbs of Colombo ; so the milder brutes, which have been partially tamed, are first hooked to the bar. They usually show a little sport at starting, but when once away the freight of passengers and post-bags is carried safely through the Pettah, and onwards at a frenzied gallop through most bewitching scenery to Kaduwella, the end of the first stage.

So far there is a choice of roads; one along the south bank of the Kelani River, where the views

"HERE ONE MAY WATCH THE QUAINT BARGES AS THEY PASS."

are surprisingly romantic and beautiful; the other, a more direct but rather less picturesque road, by which the coach usually goes.

Kaduwella is charmingly situated, and, like almost every village of importance in the Kelani Valley, has a delightful Rest-house, which is built on a steep red rock almost overhanging the river, and commanding one of the many delightful views, where the noble Kelani winds round in various directions, and displays its undulating banks, always covered with the choicest foliage. Here one may sit and watch the quaint barges and rafts as they pass, laden with produce for Colombo, or groups of natives, and cattle crossing all day long by the ferry close by. And whilst comfortably reclining in the charming verandah of this excellent hostelry, with peaceful surroundings and a sense of the most complete luxury and security, one may reflect upon the early days of the British possession, when Kaduwella was reached only by strong and narrow passes, with the very steep banks of the river to the left, and hills covered with dense jungle to the right, while in front were breastworks which could not be approached save through deep and hollow defiles.

The hostile Kadyans here made a stand against the Dutch, cutting off four hundred of their troops. The British, too, lost many men near this spot before the natives were subdued.

There is a famous Cave-Temple of the Buddhists at Kaduwella, very picturesquely situated under an enormous granite rock in the midst of magnificent trees and shrubs. It has a fine pillared hall, the bare rock forming the wall at the back. The usual colossal image of Buddha is carved in the granite, and is a good specimen of such figures.

Behind the Temple a magnificent view is to be obtained from the top of the cliff over the hilly country. The jungle is thickly inhabited by troops of black monkeys, flocks of green parrots, huge lizards like young crocodiles, and myriads of smaller creatures. Indeed, the zoologist, the botanist, and the artist need go no further for weeks;—but we must return to the Royal Mail Coach.

The quadrupeds of third-rate vice which brought us to Kaduwella have been placed in their stalls, and we now find a pair of the very first class, standing like lambs in the road. The passengers must be seated before these amiable brutes are brought blindfolded into position. All the weight that can be given to the Royal Mail is now in full requisition. The coachman takes his seat, but the running boys have still got hold of the horses. The off-side "gee" is deceived into approaching the coach, but only so far as the end of the pole, where he objects to any other position than that of facing the coachman; so while he is in that attitude, the chain is attached to the pole, and the near-side trace hooked to the bar. All efforts to move his hind quarters into position are unavailing. The near-side beast is now appealed to. He absolutely refuses to approach within some yards of Her Majesty's Mails, and so one of the tired horses, which has done the first stage, is again brought out and placed alongside of his recalcitrant successor at some distance behind the coach. This trick deceives him into thinking that he is going back to his stall. He now moves on fairly into position, and the traces are promptly hooked. The other horse remains as he was, facing the coachman. The near horse backs, but the wheels are held by coolies. The boy then slips a coir rope round his hind fetlock joints, and with a sharp friction endeavours to excite him onwards, but all to no purpose; he rears, bites at his keeper, and tries his best to back the coach into the ditch. As a last resource, a fire-stick is resorted to, and with fire at his heels he makes a frenzied bound, which starts the coach-wheels rolling, and drags the off-side horse almost into position, and off they go at full gallop, but with only three traces as yet hooked to the bar; the fourth remains in the hands of the boy who runs with the off-side horse, and this brute will not close in to the pole and give him a chance of hooking it on. After about half a mile, however, this is accomplished. The running boys, who are now getting pumped by the terrific pace, fall back, and spring on the coach-wheels, where, if the coach is full of passengers, they rest, holding on to the iron rods which support the canopy, and changing feet as the rapidly revolving hub gets hot by friction. The hubs of the coach-wheels are in this way brightly burnished by the boys springing on to them for a rest while the coach is rattling along.

The endurance of these boys in running with the horses is as amazing as their agility in springing upon the hubs of the wheels, and in bounding off to the horses again, in case of any danger, when going at the utmost pace. The coachman certainly holds a pair of reins, which are handed to him as soon as the animals can be got into going position, but compared to the work of these young horse-tamers, his duties are of little account.

The time lost in starting is soon recovered by the pace, for the more disinclined the horses have been to start, the faster do they go when once they are off; and it frequently happens that they do not slacken their furious gallop until the end of their stage is reached.

Travellers who, from a disposition to nervousness, are unable to appreciate the novel method of transit employed for the conveyance of passengers by Her

THE RIVER KELANI, FROM KARUWANELLA BRIDGE.

Majesty's Royal Mail Coach, can adopt the alternative of journeying by Bullock Cart. This mode of travelling is free from the excitement inseparable from sitting behind untamed horses, and has not only the advantage of perfect security (except, of course, when the Royal Mail comes into sight), but also gives ample time for the enjoyment of the various quaint scenes of rural life to be met with at frequent intervals along the road.

But our next journey into this enchanting district will most probably be made by rail. Such is the flourishing condition of the tea plantations and the increasing area under cultivation, that road and river no longer suffice as means of transport, and a railway running direct from the port of Colombo, through the heart of the district, is already under construction.

The large village of Hanwella is reached at the twenty-first mile-post from Colombo. It was a place of considerable consequence in the days of the Kandyan kingdom and possessed a fort commanding the principal route, both by land and water, which led from the interior of the island to Colombo. Here the last king of Kandy was defeated by Captain Pollock. Not far from this place was a palace erected for the reception of the king when on this his final expedition, and in front of it were placed the stakes on which he intended to impale the British should he capture any of them. Here many fierce battles were fought against the Kandyans, with the result of much signing of treaties and truces, which were seldom or never adhered to on the part of the native defenders of the interior. The rest-house, as at Kaduwella, commands a beautiful view of the river. Enchanting as every acre of this district is, the river views are surpassingly lovely, especially the one from Karuwanella Bridge. This is about the farthest point to which the Portuguese, and the Dutch after them, ever managed to penetrate.

The central districts of Ceylon were at that time well-nigh impenetrable owing to the density of the jungle and the entire absence of anything like good roads. Moreover, the then malarious character of the forests rendered it impossible for European troops to hold their positions for any length of time without being decimated by disease.

There are plenty of heights from which to view the diversified character of the country. Immense perpendicular ledges of rocks rise from the forest, rearing their stupendous heads above the thickets of palm and bamboo. But even the rocks of granite which appear to be upheaved in giant masses all over the forest, supply nourishment for luxuriant vegetation. The reward of human labour is, however, very apparent as we proceed further into the district of the Kelani Valley. After passing through the beautiful village of Avisawella, where, by the way, there is such a comfortable rest-house as to deserve the name of a well-appointed hotel, the scenery changes somewhat in character. It is not less bold, but the lands are more cultivated. Within the last fifteen years thousands of acres have been planted with tea, pretty bungalows have been erected on the various estates, and the whole surroundings have assumed the character of commercial enterprise.

Of the various places which the traveller will find

RUANWELLA FORD

most interesting to visit, perhaps none will prove more attractive than Ruanwella. The rest-house and its grounds, which are on the site of a ruined fort, are in themselves full of interest, and will be found so conducive to comfort as to make the visitor, who is not pressed for time very loath to leave. A fine archway, the entrance of the ancient fort, is still preserved, and forms an interesting feature in the gardens. Near to this is one of the most remarkable mango trees in Ceylon, about ninety feet high, and more than that in circumference; it is literally covered with the Thunbergia creeper, which, when in bloom, presents a magnificent appearance. In the grounds, too, are to be seen very fine specimens of Cocoa trees, graceful Papayas, many large Crotons, and a large variety of gorgeous plants which flourish here in great perfection.

The Papaya grows to a height of about fifteen or twenty feet. Its stem is slender and straight, covered by a diamond-shaped pattern, and surmounted by a crown of very prettily formed leaves, beneath which grow bunches of fruit, in shape resembling a melon. The fruit is edible, and indeed much liked by Europeans. It is said to be a very valuable aid to digestion, the amount of pepsine contained in it being highly beneficial to dyspeptics.

A pleasant stroll from the rest-house, through shady groves of areca and other palms, brings us to a part of the river which is not only very picturesque but also commercially important. Here we can see the quaint produce boats and the curiously constructed bamboo rafts being laden with freight for the port of Colombo.

From this point to Colombo the distance by water

is about sixty miles; and such is the rapidity of the current after the frequent and heavy rainfalls that these boats are able to reach Colombo in one day; the only exertion required of the boatmen being such careful steering as to keep clear of rocks, trees, and sandbanks. The return journey, however, is a more arduous task, and demands great labour and perseverance for many days.

During fine weather the river can be forded at this point, and it is quite worth while to cross over and follow the path, seen in our picture of the ford, which leads to Ruanwella estate. That such a wonderful change from jungle to orderly cultivation has been made within few years can scarcely be realised when walking along the excellently planned roads, and gazing upon the flourishing tea bushes, where a short time ago all was a mass of wild and almost impenetrable thicket.

But not only tea is to be seen; we notice profusion of delicious fruits, more especially pineapples, the finest in appearance and flavour that can be met with in Ceylon, many of them growing to a girth of twenty-four inches. Most grateful it is to feast on such delicious fruit, after the expenditure of energy demanded by the steep banks and rocky eminences over which we have climbed, and this, too, at a temperature of 90° in the shade.

Precious stones were found here in abundance in the days of the Kandyan kingdom. The name Ruanwella indicates "a place of precious stones." Among the gravel and in the sandy beds of the streams it is easy to find tiny crystals of ruby and sapphire, but without considerable plant and very careful working it is difficult to obtain anvthing of

PRODUCE BOATS ON THE KELANI AT RUANWELLA.

commercial value. Even in cases where there is no doubt of the existence of precious stones in considerable numbers, it is seldom that the European estate-owner cares to invest any of his capital in gemming operations; he prefers to apply it to uses which will yield him a more certain return.

PUNTING A PRODUCE BOAT ON THE KELANI.

CHAPTER XXII.

FROM MATALE TO TRINCOMALI.

NO European resident or visitor in Ceylon can be said to have availed himself of its greatest attractions who has not passed through the wilds of the northern parts, explored its most interesting antiquities, partaken in the sport which the almost uninhabited regions afford, and last, but not least, visited its most beautiful port—Trincomali. Its antiquities we shall pass over here, because they have been fully dealt with in another volume,* a new and cheap edition of which has recently been published; but the rest we will endeavour to accomplish.

Matale is at present the terminus of the railway towards the north. From this station there is a good road to Trincomali *via* Dambulla, the distance being one hundred miles. The country through which we shall travel is for the most part forest-clad, and inhabited chiefly by the elephant, bear, buffalo, hog, leopard, deer, and crocodile, not to mention such small fry as monkeys and plumage birds of numberless species.

---

* "The Ruined Cities of Ceylon," by Henry W. Cave. Sampson Low, Marston & Co., Ltd.

We have already described the district of Matale and may therefore pass over the first stage which brings us to Nalande. Here there is a good rest-house in which we spend a few hours during the heat of the day, resuming our journey towards Dambulla towards sunset. Upon approaching the latter village we begin to notice that the character of the country gradually changes; cultivated fields give place to

"THE VILLAGES NOW ASSUME A POVERTY-STRICKEN CHARACTER."

stretches of forest interspersed with uncultivated plains of scrub and grass land; and the villages, now few and far between, assume a poverty-stricken character compared to those nearer Kandy.

Dambulla, famous for its cave-temples, is a convenient halting-place for the night. Here we meet travellers on their way to and from the Ruined Cities, and a pleasant evening is spent, resulting in several new acquaintances. Although we are going to leave these famous antiquities alone in this volume, we may incidentally mention our conviction that the northern railway now under construction will attract all the world to Anuradhapura to see those remarkable monuments of by-gone ages which rival the marvels of ancient civilisation in the valley of the Nile. At present, considering how little known our ancient ruined cities are, and the formidable nature of the journey, the number of visitors is surprisingly large. What will it then be when half a day's railway journey from Colombo will suffice to take travellers into the heart of this mysterious region, and bring before them the wonderful remains of an old world civilisation that existed before the Christian era? This province is to be rescued from the decay due to a thousand years' desertion; its marvellous ancient irrigation works are to be restored, and, if its noble cities cannot be rebuilt, flourishing towns will, it is hoped, spring up. The periodical droughts, to which the province is subject, will again be set at nought by the restoration of the artificial lakes, and the vast wastes will give place to cultivation.

This good work, the magnitude of which can scarcely be exaggerated, was initiated in the seventies by Sir William Gregory, and has been pursued by successive governors with some success; but it has remained for Sir J. West Ridgeway to introduce the only means that, at the present day, could possibly repopulate and restore these districts to prosperity—the railway. The step was a bold one, and taken in the face of much opposition; but that the economic result will justify it I for one do not doubt.

As we proceed to Trincomali and examine the large tracts of excellent land, right and left, we see also that a branch line in this direction must in course of time inevitably follow. Indeed, there is urgent need for railway communication between Colombo and Trincomali for other reasons than the development of agriculture. The strategic advantages that would accrue are obvious even to the lay mind.

We leave Dambulla for Habarane at dawn, and as we get fairly away on the Trincomali road we notice an increase in the number of creatures that are startled by our approach. We are gradually approaching very sparsely populated districts, and begin to turn our thoughts to sport.

Habarane is really in the centre of some excellent hunting grounds, and although it is the fashion to say that game in this locality is getting scarce, there is plenty of evidence to the contrary. Here is a vast wilderness of two or three thousand square miles consisting of beautiful and valuable forest trees, interspersed with strips of open plain and vast artificial lakes, the remnants of by-gone ages, which not even the destructive tooth of time has been able to obliterate.

Let us visit one of these secluded spots not too frequently disturbed by the white man, and we shall be surprised at the countless numbers of living creatures that haunt the vicinity of a stretch of water in remote solitudes. Here a telescope may be of greater interest than a gun. Concealed beneath the shade of some beautiful tree, one may watch the habits of animals in their natural freedom. This occupation has a wonderful charm on a calm evening, with a tropical sunset glowing upon the dense jungles, whence all manner of creatures are seen to emerge and steal gently down the open glades to refresh themselves by draughts of water.

A distant sound like the blast of a horn reaches our ears, and we scan the thickets of the opposite shore: a majestic elephant is trumpeting to his herd; they obey his summons to the evening bath, and some six or eight are seen to disport themselves in the shallow waters, which they hurl over their bodies in great showers. Noises betoken the approach of

TRUMPETING TO HIS HERD.

larger numbers as the sun gradually disappears below the horizon. The shrill bark of deer, the grunt of the boar, and the screams of a myriad birds mingle as the congregation increases. The reptiles and birds are not the least interesting; crocodiles, kabaragoyas, and iguanas are present in great numbers; but the endless variety of the larger birds is the most astounding feature of these lonely shores.

There are cranes nearly six feet high; pelicans like little heaps of snow gently propelling themselves over the smooth surface of the water; the pretty little water-pheasants with their glittering heads standing upon the lotus leaves; the adjutant stalking after the reptiles; ducks innumerable and of finest plumage; teal of the most delicious species; while the gaudiest peacocks strut upon the plain. Here is a paradise for the naturalist as well as the sports-

HABARANE REST-HOUSE.

man. We must, however, proceed on our journey to Trincomali.

Every fifteen miles brings us to a rest-house, and from every rest-house we can make a sporting excursion into the jungle if that is our will. The traveller who is merely journeying to Trincomali will need very little commissariat. If he is cycling (a method of locomotion pleasant enough on this road) he will need to carry only a change of flannels, and will find most of the rest-houses provisioned with such light refreshments as he may need; or he can travel through by bullock coaches, of which there is a regular service carrying Her Majesty's Mails But if he is in search of sport and amusement on the way, a goodly supply of tinned provisions, as well as his favourite beverage, should accompany him. For this purpose a bullock cart can be hired at Matale and taken right through. Beds need not be taken unless long excursions into

A RUSH-BOTTOMED SEAT WITH THE BOTTOM RUSHEO OUT.\

the jungle are intended. The rest-houses are fully furnished with chairs, tables, and beds. We notice that the cane or rush .seats. are usually in a state of disrepair; but we make the best of such trifling circumstances. A morning's shooting, from 5.30 till noon, with the temperature at 85°, and a good tiffin at the end of it, will enable us to take our ease without the wooing of soft pillows or luxurious upholsteries.

From Habarane to Alutoya forms our next stage.

We shall admit that the road here is very beautiful, owing to the undulations and the character of the forest, which is rich in fine timber trees. Occasionally we come across a straight of a mile or two in length, and in the distance we see herds of wild hogs cross from one side to the other; here and there grey jackals put in an appearance, while monkeys and large squirrels are surprisingly numerous. Troops of wanderoos abound all the way, and at frequent intervals numbers of them leap from the branches of trees on one side of the road to those on the other. They seem to be tame as well as numerous. I suppose they are seldom shot at, although some sportsmen have boasted of the number of skins they have obtained in this district. They have good fur, and it would be tempting to kill them did not their pitiful appeals when wounded seem almost human. Anyone who has seen a wounded monkey trying to stem the flow of blood with his hand, while piteously beseeching his would-be murderer not to fire again, could not, unless by nature very cruel, level his gun again at a creature so nearly human.

After a night's rest at Alutoya, and vain attempts to bag a leopard, whose depredations have been brought to our notice, we move on to the most fascinating spot on the whole trip—the lake of Kanthalai. Many a sportsman has felt that he would not mind spending the balance of his life here. After several hours of travelling through the dense forest, it is with a shock of delight that the monotony is broken by the sudden appearance of a beautiful lake stretching away for miles to dreamy ranges of distant hills, whose beauties are reflected in its calm waters. Life and light combine to greet us as we emerge from the dense jungle. Flashes of every tint appear as the gay birds are startled by our approach. We stand enchanted by the scene. All is still save the voices of the creatures that dwell on these beautiful inland shores. Spotted deer are browsing; peacocks, airing their gaudy plumage, strut o'er the plain; the majestic elephant is enjoying his evening bath in the shallows; herds of buffaloes leave the shade of the woods to slake their thirst; grim crocodiles are basking on the shore or watching their prey; troops of chattering monkeys are sky-larking in the trees, while the stately cranes and pink flamingoes stalk the shallows. Such are the scenes that surround the tank or lake of Kanthalai.

And now let us, for a moment, go back a couple of thousand years for the origin and purpose of this gigantic artificial stonework embankment on which we stand. The history of Ceylon contains authentic records of a system of irrigation which, for engineering ingenuity and the rapidity with which gigantic works were executed, could not be surpassed by any conceivable means at the present day. We know that such works were constructed, because the evidence remains in the imperishable barriers of solid masonry that we find stretched across the valleys to secure the heavy rainfall of certain seasons; but so wonderful are they, and so intricate yet perfect the system of conveying the precious water to the field, that we cannot realise the conditions which placed such magnificent works within the sphere of the possible.

The forest now spreads over a network of these ruined lakes and tanks, tens of which are of giant

TRAVELLING WITH FULL COMMISSARIAT.

proportions, while the smaller ones number thousands. Embankments eight feet high and three hundred feet wide were carried for many miles at a stretch. The dam of one of these is eleven miles long, and is faced with steps built of twelve-feet lengths of solid granite. That on which we are standing was constructed by King Maha Sen about A.D. 275. The same monarch is said to have made no less than sixteen of the large tanks, including Minneria, which, like Kanthalai, is about twenty miles in circumference. When it is borne in mind that, in addition to the formation of the necessary embankments and sluices in this wholesale fashion, hundreds of canals for the distribution of the water formed part of the scheme, the stupendous nature of such an undertaking is manifest. Wonderful as are the remains of ancient monuments, palaces, and temples in these now deserted provinces, nothing is more impressive than the great works of irrigation, or attracts one more to the study and consideration of early Singhalese history.

How steadfast are the meteorological conditions throughout long ages of time is evidenced by these remains. The northern provinces of Ceylon must have received their rainfall thousands of years ago, as now, in deluge form during two or three months of the year; and it was necessary to secure and treasure a portion of it for use in the protracted periods of drought. It is curious in such a small country that the rain should descend with almost equal distribution throughout the year in some provinces and unequal in others. In the north-central part of Ceylon, through which we are now journeying, one-sixth of the rain for the whole year has been known to fall in a single day. The storms of this district have been well described by Major Forbes, who, in writing of his journey to Trincomali in 1833, says: "Five miles beyond Dambool we crossed the bed of the Meerisagona-oya, at a ford which for nine months of the year is only a space covered with sand; but the banks of this stream, above and below, were about eight feet in height, the perpendicular sides being supported by matted roots of trees.

"Although the Meerisagona-oya was now and for months had been without a drop of water in its channel, I have known it impassable even to horses for eight days together: detentions on this road from the swelling of the streams usually occur previous to the setting-in of the north-east monsoon in November. The rains generally commence towards the end of September with heavy showers; after a week of this unsettled weather, rain falls in torrents for half the day, the remainder being bright sunshine. Previous to the fall of these quotidian deluges, the sky in the quarter from whence they approach becomes gradually darkened upward from the horizon, and appears of an inky hue, so dense that the distant hills look less solid than the advancing curtain of clouds. The plains seem lost in dull shadows; and the mountains are lighted with a lurid gleam of dusky red that escapes from the open part of the heavens. Every second this clear space, with its pale, cold blue sky, is visibly contracted by dark swollen masses of vapour, which are gradually subduing the sickly lights that linger on the highest pinnacles. At first, during these symptoms, there is an oppressive calm, under which everything in nature seems to droop: the leaves hangs listless on the boughs; the beasts are in the forest; the birds seek shelter in the covert; numerous flocks of white cranes following each other in lines, or forming themselves in angles, alone attract the eye as they seek new ground and prepare for the approaching storm. Before a breath of air is felt, tiny whirlwinds are seen beneath the bushes, twirling round a few light withered leaves, or trundling them along the footpath. These fairy hurricanes are succeeded by a rushing sound among the trees overhead, accompanied by the rustling and falling of decayed leaves; then a gentle and refreshing air suddenly gives place to cold breezes, gusts, and squalls, until heavy drops of rain crowd into descending sheets of water, transforming steep paths into cataracts, and broad roads into beds of rivers. Before the murky curtain that is closing over the sky flickers a cold misty veil, and a dull vapour rolls in advance along the ground; these appearances arise from the raindrops splashing on the dusty ground, or jostling and splintering as they descend from the teeming darkness. On a particular occasion, being surprised by one of these avalanches of rain, I returned to my house at Matale; but, with my horse, had to swim across a stream that I had passed only two hours before, when the water was not three inches deep."

The storms being restricted to one season, we have no difficulty in arranging to make our trips in certain fine weather. But we are digressing at great length, and must now proceed on our journey from the spot where we halted at the first glimpse of Kanthalai.

The great causeway extends for upwards of a mile, and is bordered with beautiful trees. It is faced with enormous blocks of granite regularly laid, but covered with turf to the water's edge. Near the Trincomali end a capacious rest-house for the accommodation of large parties of sportsmen and travellers stands on the brink, so near the verge as to be insecure. Our picture shows the porchway, which has been shored up, and the heavy roof replaced by palm-thatch, lest the whole should

ON THE BANKS OF KANTHALAI.

precipitate into the lake. In the foreground stands a famous shikaree, whose ears and eyes are sharp and keen for every sound and sight of the jungle. Whether it be pig, buffalo, deer, or elephant you want, he knows the locality of a herd as if he were its keeper. The fields, which are irrigated from the lake, are unrivalled as snipe grounds. The bags that are made by officers from the garrison and warships at Trincomali are sometimes so great that

I hesitate to pen the number lest I should tempt the incredulous reader to offer criticism in terms more common than polite.

We have now only one more stage to Trincomali —26 miles of the same undulated forest road.

REFRESHING

TRINCOMALI HARBOUR, FROM ADMIRALTY HOUSE.

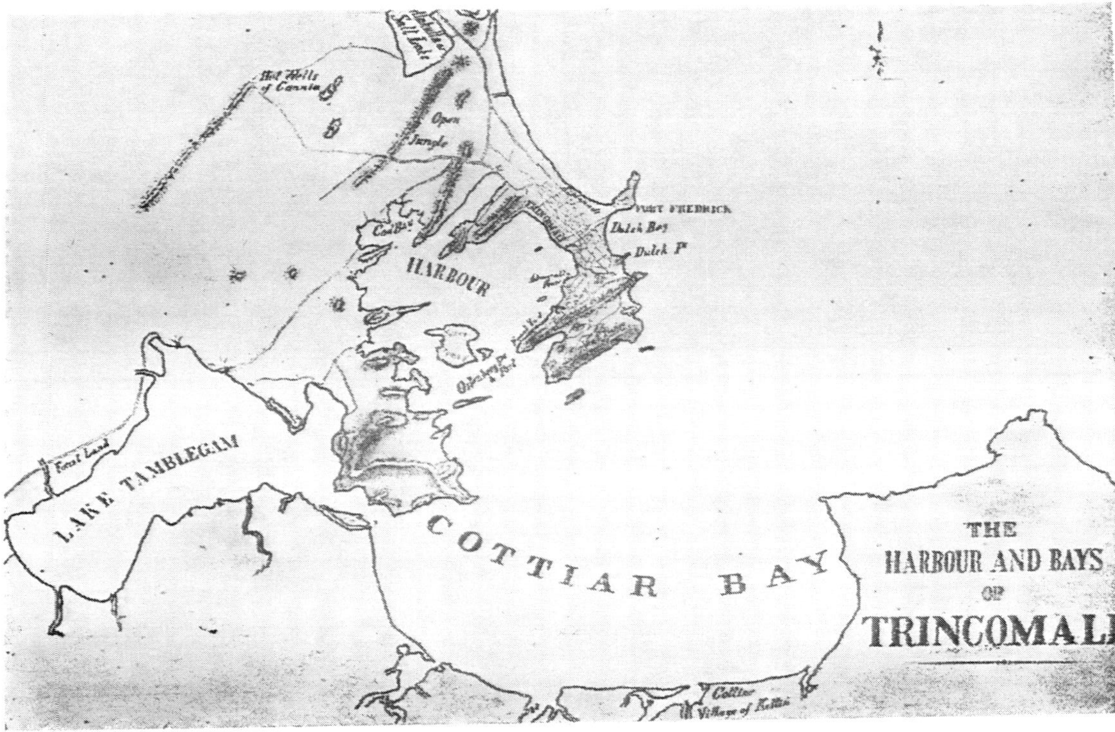

THE
HARBOUR AND BAYS
OF
TRINCOMALI
COTTIAR BAY
HARBOUR
LAKE TAMBLEGAM
FORT FREDRICK
Dutch Bay
Dutch Pt
Hot Wells
of Cannia
Open
Jungle
Cottiar
Village of Kottia
Forest Land

CHAPTER XXIII.

TRINCOMALI.

THERE are some five or six magnificent harbours in the world, and Trincomali is one of them. Its lovely scenery is of a character so extensive that no realistic representation can be made upon paper, and we must therefore content ourselves with the limited capacity of the camera to produce, in parts only, what we conceive to be a thing of superb beauty as a whole. Situated on the north-east of the island, it faces the Bay of Bengal and overlooks the whole eastern coast of India. The entrance, which faces south-east, is guarded by two projecting headlands, approaching to within about seven hundred yards of each other. When it is borne in mind that the monsoons blow from the north-east and south-west the importance of this feature is obvious. The rocky headlands have a beautiful effect upon the landscape, which is made up of a placid expanse of water dotted with wooded islets that seem to float on its surface; rich tropical forest covering the acclivities that border its coasts, and a distant background of lofty mountains.

The form of the harbour is irregular, and the

numerous indents of its coast line supply many a charming feature. Some of the islands are romantic in appearance as well as association, and notably amongst them Sober Island, a favourite resort of the officers of the East Indies Squadron, who have built a ward-room, billiard-room, and gun-room upon it. The walls of the gun-room have been highly decorated by its youthful members. This island is

AVENUE ON SOBER ISLAND.

very thickly wooded, as may be seen from our pictures; the avenue, which we depict, possessing almost the only cleared space, while rich and luxurious vegetation flourishes from shore to summit.

Trincomali is regarded as a very important naval station, and as such it is strongly fortified; but as a commercial port it has not developed, for the simple reason that the cinnamon trade, so attractive to the early colonists, could only be carried on at Colombo; and later, when the English gained possession of the interior, the country in the west was found to be the more cultivated, while the north-east was almost deserted by man and covered with dense forest; moreover, the long droughts to which the northern provinces were subject rendered their cultivation apparently hopeless. Later than this another circumstance greatly influenced the development of Colombo as the commercial port: the Suez Canal

OBER ISLAND.

brought the shipping for the colonies in the direction of Ceylon, and as a consequence the western harbour suddenly assumed immense importance by reason of its convenience as a junction and port of call. So Trincomali by accident of its position has missed that service to commerce which, if it had been on the south-west coast, would have been immense. But its value for naval purposes cannot be over-estimated. The flag-ship of the Eastern fleet is generally in the harbour for several months of the year, and the Admiral, his family, staff, and officers of the ship are considered part of the permanent society of the place.

Our principal view of the harbour is taken from the drawing-room verandah of the Admiral's house. It is a charming house, commanding the best views across the harbour. We have just now seen Admiral Kennedy's testimony to its comfort and salubrity in his new book "Hurrah! for the life of a Sailor." He says: "For those who do not mind tropical heat Trincomali is a pleasant resort, and certainly Admiralty House is the place to enjoy it. Designed by a ship's carpenter, it is built so as to catch the sea-breeze, which sweeps through the spacious rooms. A broad flight of steps leads up to the dining- and drawing-rooms, and the bed-rooms are on each side. On the ground-floor are offices, and servants' apartments, and over all a flat roof from which a fine view of the harbour is obtained, and a cool retreat to smoke the post-prandial cigar before turning in." The disposition of the ornamental shrubs and trees renders a photograph of the front of the house impossible, so we must content ourselves with a view of the back taken from beneath the finest banyan tree in Ceylon, which is in the grounds of the house.

Amongst the beautiful trees to be found in Trincomali this grand specimen of the *Ficus Indica* stands pre-eminent. It is difficult for anyone who has not seen a banyan tree to realise that all the stems and branches visible in our two little photographs are parts of one tree. As the branches grow and become too weighty for the parent stems they throw

ADMIRALTY HOUSE (BACK VIEW).

down pendent aërial roots which strike the ground and become themselves supporting stems for the immense branches. It will be seen that some of these stems rival even the main trunk in size, notably the one on the extreme left of our first picture. In our second picture only a portion of the complete tree is visible, but enough is given to show how the shoots have reached the ground and grown into large supporting stems, enveloping the original trunk and producing the appearance of a miniature forest. The circumference of the tree, which thus appears as a whole grove, extends to several hundred feet, and its o'erspreading branches would easily shelter a thousand people.

These trees are greatly in favour with the flying-foxes, especially when ripe with seed, which serves as a dainty nocturnal feast to these curious bird-beasts. They sleep in them by day, suspended from the boughs by their claws, which at nightfall they unhook, and spreading their heavy wings they fly around in large numbers, making no little noise in foraging exploits. It is quite easy on a moonlit night to bring them down with a gun. If not killed outright they are by no means gentle creatures to deal with, and the help of a hunting knife is not to be despised in view of the fact that they fight violently with their huge claws and sharp teeth. The size of their bodies is about as large as that of a cat, their wings measuring about four feet from tip to tip.

There is a very picturesque carriage road winding along the northern and eastern portions of the harbour, and many are its pretty nooks and corners. We could reproduce a large number, but must

BANYAN TREE, SHOWING THE PARENT STEM.

THE SAME TREE, SHOWING SOME OF THE SUPPORTING STEMS.

THE GARDEN SLOPE OF ADMIRALTY HOUSE.

A PICTURESQUE CARRIAGE ROAD

content ourselves with four. In the first we see the garden slope of Admiralty House, where on reception days the latest Parisian costumes that have reached Trincomali are donned by the all too few ladies in residence. This is the scene of pastimes, too, and many a bullet has chipped the rock visible in our picture instead of breaking the bottle placed there for its reception.

Our photograph on the opposite page gives a very good idea of the character of this pretty road, and we particularly notice here how land-locked the harbour is. We are looking towards the mouth, in the direction of the full-rigged ship which is discharging coal at the wharf. On the left is the extensive hill known as Fort Ostenburg, commanding the entrance of the harbour. Military barracks are just visible amongst the trees. The buildings at the water's edge are, of course, naval, and we are supposed to know very little about these or the forts which are bristling with guns in every commanding position. It is not within our province to say more than that a warm reception awaits any enemy who might endeavour to enter here.

Our next picture (page 40[illegible]) is a little bay, near the Naval Hospital. It needs no comment, and is introduced merely to show how pretty are the little indentations of the harbour shores.

If we proceed a few yards beyond this position and then look back we get a lovely view, in which the palmyra tree figures amongst the aloes on the right, and Snake Island, one of the many little wooded islets, is seen in mid-distance.

To the north of the harbour there is a horse-shoe shaped bay, guarded on one side by the rocky

BAY NEAR THE NAVAL HOSPITAL.

DUTCH POINT.

BAY BETWEEN DUTCH POINT AND FORT FREDERICK, TAKEN FROM "THE RESIDENCY" ON DUTCH POINT.

FORT FREDERICK.

headland known as Dutch Point, and on the other by Fort Frederick, which is a peninsula with narrow isthmus, but presenting a wide and bold front of precipitous rocks about a mile out to sea. Our illustrations will explain. The town of Trincomali is at the bend of the horse-shoe. It has a fine "Maidan" of some three hundred acres to the sea front. This forms the recreation ground of the residents, and includes golf links and a good carriage drive. Facing the bay are a few good residences, including the Vicarage,

NAVAL COMMISSIONER'S HOUSE.

the Rest-house, and the magnificent residence of the officer in charge of the dockyard and naval stores, known as "Naval Commissioner's House." It will be easy for the reader to obtain a good idea of this part of Trincomali by a careful glance at our photographs.

If we look at "Dutch Point", we may see the roof of the Residency, the official quarters of the Government Agent, who acts as both civil and judicial administrator. The grounds of this house are very romantic, and stretch around the headland, where the little bays and crevices afford us many pretty pictures. If we now look from the porch of the Residency, shown in our next picture, we have the whole bay before us, Fort Frederick being just out of the picture in the distance on the right. The white dome of the Roman Catholic Church, which we see by looking through the porchway, indicates the direction of the native town, while the "Maidan" begins where the palm trees abruptly end, on the shore, in the middle of the picture.

Another small view taken from the garden of the Residency shows how the peninsula which forms Fort Frederick stretches out to sea, thus forming this deep and beautiful bay. Fort Frederick is in itself very picturesque, being diversified by rocks, woodland, and glade. Herds of wild deer dwell there, in the neighbourhood of barracks and guns, and lend a charm to the somewhat rugged features of the landscape.

We must pause here for a few moments. This place is of great antiquity, and many graceful legends are interwoven with its history. We have noticed that Fort Frederick widens and increases in elevation from the isthmus at its entrance until it presents a bold front to the deep sea. The brow of its headland is a mighty crag rising from deep water in a sheer precipice, to the height of four hundred feet. Such an unusual feature of the landscape was certain to attract the reverence of the imaginative Hindus, and although the Singhalese may have regarded this as a holy place for centuries before the time of Buddha, when they themselves were Brahmans, and may have built shrines there, it is certain that the Malabars who invaded Ceylon in early times appropriated it, and built a stupendous shrine to Siva, which, until it was demolished by the Portuguese in 1622, was known as "The Temple of a Thousand Columns," and was the resort of pilgrims from all parts of India. There is now left only the bare site of the magnificent temple; and as the crowds of Hindus flock thither to worship at the Saami Rock, which is all the ruthless cruelty of the Portuguese left them, one cannot help feeling some pity for them in having their most revered shrine demolished without the slightest reason that could have appealed to them. What their feelings must have been towards the Portuguese makes one shudder to think. No wonder that the Portuguese proved useless conquerors! We know that the Tamil Hindus meted out similar treatment to the Buddhist Singhalese in olden times; but we should have expected the methods of the Portuguese, professing Christianity, to have been less brutal in the seventeenth century. We shall see that the site of this sacrilege is still held in the profoundest veneration.

For many years after the British took possession of the Fort, the Hindus, who had been debarred from approaching the sacred spot by the Portuguese and the Dutch, were allowed the privilege of making a pilgrimage to it once a year, and, although the site has increased in military importance, this favour of the authorities has been extended, instead of withdrawn, as it would have been by any other nation, until the pilgrimages have increased to an allowance of two a week. The high caste devotees now attend on Friday and the low on Monday. The processions take place at sunset, and there is no interference with them save a sufficiency of military

THE SAAMI ROCK AT TRINCOMALI.

sentries to see that no one deviates from the permitted route or remains within the Fort after the ceremonies are over.

Having taken up our position on the only jutting crag that gives us an unobstructed view of the Saami Rock, from ocean to pinnacle, we await the arrival of the worshippers, who appear gradually, both men and women, each bearing offerings of fruit, milk, palm blossoms, grain, and flowers. They take up positions whence they can gaze upon the ceremonies to be performed by the officiating priest, who, with several attendants, descends to the utmost ledge, a giddy height, where naught but the fathomless ocean stretches beneath his feet. Here he pours out libations, chants a weird litany, and taking each gift casts it into the mighty deep. He then kindles a fire, which he thrice raises above his head in a brazen censer, while all the worshippers raise their arms heavenward. The burnt offerings are reduced to ashes, which are then smeared upon the foreheads of the worshippers, and the ceremony is over. The situation as seen in our photograph is strikingly impressive, and amongst the numberless religious ceremonies of the East none is more profoundly solemn. The pouring of libations and the sacrifice of burnt offerings on a spot where the handiwork of the Creator is visible on all sides in its most wonderful aspects, is worthy of a much more enlightened people, and commands our sympathy.

It might seem that minds capable of such devotion would be easily influenced by Western civilisation, and that the darker forms of Brahmanism would yield to the missionary's efforts. But it must be borne in mind that the proportion of Europeans to natives here is one to a thousand, and that there is a proud fanatic spirit bred in the very bone of the Hindu, which renders any human effort to convert him a Herculean task. We can only hope that the education of the young will gradually introduce enlightened ideas, and as the European population increases, Christianity will gradually triumph over the lower forms of religion that have such a firm hold upon the Indian people.

We cannot leave the Saami Rock without reference to an event of pathetic interest, commemorated by the monument which surmounts its loftiest crag. As will be observed in our picture, it is a solitary pillar, probably one of the thousand columns of the demolished temple, and on it is engraved :

TOT GEDAGHTENIS
VAN FRANCINA VAN REEDE
IUF° VAN MYDREGT DESEN
A° 1687: 24 APRIL
OPGEREGT

Francina Van Reede was a Dutch maiden of high birth, the daughter of a gentleman holding a responsible position in the Dutch service. She was betrothed to an officer in the army, stationed at Trincomali, to whom she was desperately attached ; but he proved faithless, and embarked on a vessel bound for Europe. The fair one watched the movements of the ship from the Saami Rock. To get clear of the coast the vessel had to tack and pass parallel to the precipice on which the love-sick maiden stood. For a few moments she gazed distractedly towards her false lover, when suddenly the swift vessel turned from her towards a foreign land, and she plunged from the dizzy height.

We have already referred to the beautiful bungalow which is at present occupied by Mr. Marcus W. Millet, the officer in charge of the Naval Dockyard. Our illustrations would be incomplete without this, which is one of the many pleasant features of Trincomali. It was built by a merchant at the beginning of the century and bought by the Government as a residence for the Naval Commissioner. Its present occupant is a famous sportsman, who has probably exploited the wild hunting grounds of the neighbourhood more thoroughly than anyone. By his courtesy we pay a visit to the savannahs of Tamblegam, where game of all kinds abounds. This is a very popular resort for a day's shooting, and, moreover, combines a water-excursion of the most delightful character. A start is made at 6.30 a.m. by a short drive to the pier. Thence we sail across the beautiful harbour to a neck of land which divides it from the great Tamblegam lake. Here we leave the boat and walk for ten minutes through scrub. Another boat awaits us on the Tamblegam shore, and we sail away again across a fine expanse of shallow water famous alike for its crocodiles and its luscious oysters. Upon arriving at the chosen ground for the day's sport we disembark, fix up a tent as seen in our picture, and for the rest of the day make shooting excursions, alternated by intervals for refreshment. The last-named part of the programme is by no means the least pleasant, especially when, in addition to the luxuries conveyed thither in the boat, the servants add fine crabs caught and cooked on the spot, and unlimited oysters, as fine as any in the world, fished up and served *ad libitum.* The return journey at sunset is a delightful ending to a perfectly enjoyable day.

It would not be true to say that such excursions await everyone who visits Trincomali, because the nautical and commissariat arrangements of Mr. Millet are such as few can command; but that sport

UNDER CANVAS AT TAMBLEGAM.

awaits everybody who likes to go for it is certain. It is this fact that, in the opinion of the military and other officials stationed there, counterbalances the disadvantage of isolation from the rest of the colony. There is a peculiar charm in the circumstance that between this beautiful place and any other lies a stretch of wild and unpeopled land, where almost every kind of wild animal that exists in the island can be found. Elephants, leopards, bears, boars, buffaloes, deer, monkeys, crocodiles, are all within a day's march and many within an hour's ride.

The neighbourhood of Trincomali presents yet another feature which is within our province to mention, and is noteworthy in connection with the theory held by some that the deep harbour is on the site of a submerged volcano. At Kanya, near a range of wooded hills eight miles north of the harbour, there are some hot wells, seven in number, differing in degrees of temperature from 100° to 110°. These springs have naturally given rise to various legends amongst the natives, who regard them with superstitious reverence, and account for their origin in the following fable. To delay the King Rawana, and thus prevent the success of one of his undertakings, Vishnu appeared in the form of an old man, and falsely informed the king that Kanya (the virgin-mother of Rawana) had died. On hearing this, Rawana determined to remain and perform the usual solemnities for deceased relatives, whenever he could find water for the requisite ablutions. Vishnu having ascertained his wishes, disappeared at the spot, and caused the hot springs to burst forth. From the solemnities then performed in honour of Kanya, the springs have ever since retained her name.*

It will be seen from our map that to the south of Trincomali harbour there is a very large bay almost as land-locked as the harbour itself. In the days of sailing ships, and especially in early times when Ceylon was the great emporium of the Eastern world, Cottiar Bay, as this great neighbour of Trincomali

* From an account given by Major Forbes, 78th Highlanders.

is called, was a place of immense importance, compared with which Trincomali itself was insignificant; the reason doubtless being that it afforded sufficient depth of water for the vessels of those days, while ingress and egress under sail were much easier than through the narrower entrance of the adjoining harbour.

At the present day Cottiar interests the traveller as the scene of the capture of the commander and

THE WHITE MAN'S TREE.

crew of a British ship by the King of Kandy in the year 1659. This misfortune, deplorable in itself, has for us a literary interest. To it, as a primary cause, we are indebted for our knowledge of the condition of the interior of Ceylon and its people under native rule in the middle of the seventeenth century. But we will embark for Cottiar and there tell the story under the grand old Tamarind tree that survives to commemorate the event referred to.

We sail across the lovely bay, and in a couple of hours find ourselves anchored on the very spot where the good ship *Anne* lost her ill-fated crew two and a half centuries ago. We are near the mouth of the Mahawelli-ganga, up which we sail for about half a mile. Here we proceed ashore, and our interest is arrested by a strange monument of white stone erected against the gnarled stem of a magnificent old tree. We approach and read the inscription :—

THIS IS THE WHITE MAN'S TREE
UNDER WHICH ROBERT KNOX
WAS CAPTURED
A.D. 1659.

Robert Knox was the son of the captain of the *Anne.* He and his father, with fourteen of the crew, were treacherously seized by the natives and carried captive to the King at Kandy. Here they were distributed into various villages; but Robert and his father were permitted to be together. Father and son were sent to Bandarakoswatta, a village thirty-five miles north-west of Kandy, where they soon fell sick from malarial fever and the poor captain winged his flight. Robert tells us in the following touching words how he buried his father: "With my own hands I wrapped him up ready for the grave, myself being very sick and weak, and, as I thought, ready to follow after him. Having none but a black boy with me I bade him ask the people of the town for help to carry my father to the grave, because I could not understand their language, who immediately brought forth a great rope they used to tie their cattle withal, therewith to drag him by the neck into the woods, saying they could afford me no other help unless I would pay for it. This insolency of the heathen grieved me much to see; neither could I, with the boy alone, do what was necessary, having not wherewithal to dig a grave, and the ground being very dry and hard; yet it was some comfort to me that I had so much ability as to hire one to help, which at first I would not have spared to have done had I known their meaning."

Robert was now alone amongst the natives, and so remained, for the most part, during his nineteen years' captivity. He occasionally came across some of the crew and lived with two of them for a considerable time, but they, being less refined in their tastes than he, found wives amongst the native women and settled down to native life and customs. Robert, on the other hand, preserved his dignity, found great consolation in religion, clung to the hope of escape, and stored up in his memory every fact that he could grasp about the country and its inhabitants. At length these virtues had their reward; he escaped, and lived to present his countrymen and all posterity with what Tennent justly describes as "the most faithful and life-like portraiture that was ever drawn of a semi-civilised but remarkable people." His book, published in the reign of Charles the Second, is the greatest and most lasting monument of this "gentlest of historians and meekest of captives." He brought nothing away upon his back or in his purse, yet did he transport the whole kingdom in his head, and by writing and publishing his observations he did a literary service to posterity, which will preserve his name for many more centuries.

CHAPTER XXIV

JAFFNA.

ALTHOUGH the northern province of Ceylon is for the most part a wild and uncultivated region, Jaffna, its extreme district, has the opposite characteristics, being not only cultivated to the utmost extent, but also densely populated. The history of the almost forsaken country which lies between this fertile region and the tea districts has been dealt with in another volume, and we shall therefore here confine our attention to the peninsula of Jaffna only. The journey thither can be made by road, and will soon be possible by rail; but for the present it will suit our purpose better to voyage from Trincomali to Point Pedro, and thence to cycle across the peninsula.

Point Pedro is almost the extreme point of Ceylon. It cannot boast of a harbour; but the coral reef which guards the shore affords shelter and a safe anchorage. The little town is neat and trim. We notice at once that care is bestowed on the upkeep of roads, bungalows, and gardens, suggesting an industrious population. It derives its importance from the circumstance that the town of Jaffna, on the western side of the peninsula, is never approachable by ships within some miles, owing to the way in which the water shoals towards the coast; while in the south-west monsoon ships of eight or ten feet draft cannot approach near enough to receive and discharge cargo at this port. At such a time Point Pedro and Kankesanturai, although open roadsteads, are invaluable anchorages.

The whole peninsula is peopled by Tamils, the

ENTRANCE TO THE FORT, JAFFNA.

Dravidian race of southern India, who have doubtless occupied it for upwards of two thousand years. They differ greatly from the Singhalese in being industrious agriculturists; and considering how entirely they have brought Jaffna under cultivation, and how active they are, it is somewhat surprising that they have kept within the territory of this one district, while so much land immediately to the south of them lies waste. There is no doubt, however, that the railway, now in course of construction, is intended to entice them southwards, and that the deserted fields and solitudes which lie in this direction will be re-tilled by them when they see new markets opened by rapid and direct means of communication.

No sooner do we set our foot upon the soil of Jaffna than we perceive a change from the rest of Ceylon in climate, productions, and people. The air is dry, there is an absence of streams, the Palmyra palm takes the place of the coconut, and the fields present the appearance of carefully kept market gardens, watered from wells—a contrast to the wild and untended luxuriance of the low-lying districts in the south. There are no undulations in the land; all is one level and unbroken stretch of cultivation save where shallow lagoons have been formed by inlets from the sea.

The most striking feature of the landscape is the Palmyra palm, which flourishes in the greatest profusion all over the peninsula. Many pages might be written about this most valuable tree and the hundreds of uses to which its products are applied. We must, however, be satisfied with a very condensed account. Like the Talipot which we described on page 85, the Palmyra has a straight stem which reaches the height of seventy to eighty feet, and similarly also it has broad fan-like leaves. Its wood is hard and its fruit, which grows in huge clusters, supplies about one-fourth of the food of the poorer inhabitants. The sugar of the Palmyra, called by the natives *jaggery*, is its most important product. This is obtained by bruising the embryo flowers. The spathes are first bound with thongs to prevent expansion and cause the sap to exude, and then earthenware chatties are suspended to collect the juice which, in response to frequent bruisings, continues to flow for some four or five months. Once in three years only the fruit is allowed to form, lest the tree should die from the continued artificial extraction of its juices. The liquor needs only to be boiled down to the consistency of syrup, when, upon cooling, it becomes jaggery without any further preparation.

When the fruit is allowed to ripen it forms in beautiful clusters on each flower stem, of which there are seven or eight on a tree. The fruit contains seeds embedded in pulp, and from these food is extracted in various forms. One method is to plant the seeds and take the germs in their first stage of growth; these, after being dried in the sun and dressed, form a luscious vegetable. The germs can also be reduced to flour, which is considered a great delicacy. The shells of the seeds make splendid fuel, engendering a great heat. The wood, being very hard and durable, is excellent material for roofing. The leaves are in very great request for thatch, fencing, mats, baskets, fans, umbrellas, and many other purposes. In earlier times they were almost universally used as parchment for manuscript books and legal documents.

Next the tobacco fields attract our attention. Great care is bestowed upon this product, which flourishes so well that the Jaffnese have for many years regarded it as their most important staple. The irrigation of the tobacco fields, as well as the extensive fruit and flower gardens which everywhere abound, is primitive and peculiar. Water is obtained exclusively from wells; and it is raised after sunset by labourers in the following manner: A horizontal lever in the form of a log of wood about fifteen feet long is so attached to a high post that it will act like the see-saw beloved of village children in Europe; a woven basket of Palmyra leaves is attached to the end of the lever over the well. A couple of coolies then play see-saw by walking to and fro on the log, making the basket descend and return again full of water by the continued motion of their bodies. Thousands of coolies thus draw water during the night, and others distribute it over the fields and gardens. Sometimes one cooly is sufficient for the lever. Another labourer stands near and directs the bucket in its ascent, and empties it into the necessary channel by which it is conducted to the plants.

We are amazed no less at the orderly and cleanly cultivation than the variety of it. Every kind of "curry-stuff" seems to grow in Jaffna, which also produces the best fruits of the island. A large export trade is done in them, which compensates for the importation of rice. Dry grains are easily grown; but rice, which requires much water, is unsuited to the soil and climate.

There is no town in Ceylon which still bears the impress of the Dutch occupation in its general features so completely as Jaffna. This is doubtless owing to the architecture of its most prominent buildings—the Fort and the bungalows. The Fort was beautifully built of coral, and it shows no signs of decay at the present day. Some idea of the masonry can be gathered from our little pictures. Within its enclosure are several fine buildings: a massive church in the form of a Greek cross, the

Queen's House, occupied by the Governor of the colony upon official visits, Government offices and police quarters. There are now very few Presbyterians resident in Jaffna, and in consequence the church has become disused and its furniture removed. The size of the church and the large number of tombs of Dutch officials testify to the importance of Jaffna in the Dutch period.

The visitor to Jaffna can make himself very com-

THE REST-HOUSE JAFFNA.

fortable at the excellent rest-house which we depict here. It faces an open park-like space, intersected with good roads and fine avenues of Suriya and other trees.

Altogether the town of Jaffna gives us a favourable impression. Its bungalows are spacious, well-built and very clean; its streets are wide and well tended, while its gardens and commons are so well-kept as to suggest that there are no idle folk amongst the inhabitants. In fact, everyone is very busy at Jaffna and we find that about as much work is thoroughly done there for one rupee as in Colombo is half done for double the amount.

We have referred to the race that inhabits Jaffna as one of agriculturists; but we also find industrious artizans working in the carpentry, jewellery and other trades. The goldsmiths are ingenious and have formed very distinct styles and patterns that are

THE DUTCH FORT AT JAFFNA.

peculiar to them. Their bangles, brooches, chains, and rings are beautiful in design and workmanship, while their tools are of the most primitive order and few in number.

There are many other things of considerable interest in Jaffna which we must pass over here; but with which the visitor will make himself acquainted. Our steamer is at anchor six miles from the shore, and as we proceed towards it we dwell upon the striking scenes which the little peninsula has afforded us, and contrast them in our minds with the wild and uncultivated, yet beautiful lands further south. We cannot help feeling that the latter are too common in Ceylon. We are glad to have visited the fertile plains of Jaffna, and to have journeyed over its excellent roads and through its smiling fields, Economic qualities are, after all, more desirable than scenery.

TAKING THEIR PHOTOGRAPHS.

CHAPTER XXV.

RAMESERAM.

ON our voyage from Jaffna to Colombo we pass through the very narrow strait known as Paumben Passage. Here Ceylon is almost joined to India by a curious line of rocks and islands. It will be seen from our map that the mainland of the continent sends forth a promontory which almost reaches the sacred island of Rameseram. From this a ridge of rocks, known as Adam's Bridge, extends to Manaar, an island of sand-drifts cut off from the coast of Ceylon only by fordable shallows. Whether Ceylon was ever actually joined to India either by nature or artifice is a matter of conjecture; but the possibility of either is easy to demonstrate. The name Adam's Bridge is insignificant, and is due to a legend of the Arabs, who were traders on this coast in very early times. They believed that Adam lived in Ceylon after his banishment from Paradise; that he journeyed thence to Mecca and brought Eve back with him. It was natural that he should have gone to and fro by this passage as there were no ships in those days. So they called it Adam's Bridge. The legends of the Brahmans are not quite so simple.

By them Rama is said to have employed the monkey gods to form this footway in order that he might invade Ceylon with an army. There were quarrels and jealousies about it, sometimes assuming serious proportions, as when Nala stretched out his *left* hand to receive the immense rocks brought by Hanuman. This indignity so roused the anger of the latter that he raised a mountain to hurl at Nala when Rama interposed and appeased him by explaining that, although gifts might not be received with the left hand, it was the custom of masons so to receive materials for building.

We are not disinclined to accept the theory that Paumben Passage was once blocked by an artificial causeway, over which millions of pilgrims came to visit the sacred Rameseram. The passage only fifty years ago was so shallow that no ships could pass through; but was about that time deepened sufficiently for vessels of ten to twelve feet draft.

Although Rameseram is not part of Ceylon, we find it easily accessible, since the steamers of the Ceylon Steamship Company pass through the Paumben Passage weekly, and obligingly anchor to allow passengers an opportunity of visiting the island. We have said that it is a sacred island, and we shall now proceed to verify this statement by a complete exploration.

If we except a long spit of land which runs out to Adam's Bridge, the extent of the island is about seven miles by three. Upon setting out from Paumben, a broad road, paved with smooth slabs of granite and shaded by beautiful trees, stretches eastward through the island, ending in the entrance of a remarkable temple, one of the most ancient and revered in all India. On either side, at frequent intervals throughout the whole distance of seven miles, there are substantially built ambalams or rest-houses for pilgrims, fine baths with granite steps descending into them from all sides, and temples beautifully built of hewn stone. Every tree as well as building is dedicated to the purposes of religion. Even the soil is so sacred that no plough may break it; and no animal wild or tame may be killed upon it. The magnificence of this superb highway is, however, in ruin; but why it should be so we are unable to ascertain. The paving-stones are displaced, and most of the temples are in ruins, while the ambalams show signs of better days, not long past. The condition of the whole indicates that about a century ago all these were in beautiful order. At the present day, however, the great temple of Rama appears to be the only building upon which attention is lavished.

No idea of this structure can be gained from the exterior, the only part visible being the lofty pagoda which forms the entrance. The rest of the temple is enclosed within high walls, extending round an area of eight hundred by six hundred feet. The interior consists of a large number of galleries of grand extent and dimensions, some of them running through the whole length of the temple, and others to right and left for hundreds of feet. All of them are ornamented with rows of massive pillars carved with statues of gods and departed heroes. Our photograph of one small portion of a gallery is fairly representative of the whole, which extends for many thousands of feet, and surrounds the *sanctum sanctorum*, an oblong rectangular space into which the unbeliever may not penetrate. No entreaties will avail to obtain admittance into this sanctified place. The nautch girls who are dancing and chanting within may come and perform to us outside; but we may not approach the shrines.

We are astonished at the Hindu grandeur of the temple, and we are naturally curious about the apparent neglect of the large number of smaller

PORTION OF ONE OF THE GALLERIES OF RAMESERAM.

temples on the island. This, we are told, is due to the falling off in the number of pilgrims, and consequently in contributions, since the British prohibition of human sacrifice. A century ago, when enormous cars, surmounted by images of the gods, were dragged along the paved ways by hundreds of frantic devotees, many in their frenzy hurled themselves beneath the massive wheels. It is also related to us that when the great car of Juggernaut was periodically brought from Madura across the Paumben causeway the sacrifices were enormous, and the number of pilgrims attracted at such times was a great source of income to the temples. We should like to think that the decay which we have observed was due to enlightenment and education rather than British law and might; but be that as it may, we are quite gratified to see the temples in ruins if the circumstance indicates the discontinuance of barbarous customs in however small degree.

Mannar is scarcely worth a visit. It presents a dreary aspect in comparison with the rest of Ceylon, notwithstanding that in earlier times it was regarded as a place of considerable commercial importance from its proximity to India and the yield of its pearl fisheries. It is now famous only for its baobab trees (*adansonia digitata*), which must have been imported many centuries ago from the coast of Africa; but by whom and for what purpose is a mystery. The peculiarity of this monstrous tree is in its shapeless massive stem, whose circumference is equal to the height of the tree.

From Paumben we reach Colombo by steamer in about twelve hours.

MORATUWA MAIDS.

CHAPTER XXVI.

THE SOUTH COAST.

THE seaside railway, from Colombo to Matara, affords every facility for visiting the villages and towns of the south coast, where Singhalese life pure and simple can be seen to greater advantage than anywhere else in Ceylon. Here is to be found the purely Singhalese section of the inhabitants of the island, a circumstance due to the fact that the low-lands of the south were not invaded by the Malabars, who in early times conquered and held possession of the northern provinces for long periods, with the result of a considerable commixture of the Aryan and Dravidian races. A full description of all the interesting places in the south, with adequate reference to notable events in their history, especially that of the Dutch occupation, would swell this volume to an inconvenient size; we must therefore content ourselves here with brief notice of a few of them. Twelve miles south of Colombo lies the large and exceedingly picturesque village of Moratuwa, the inhabitants of which apply themselves almost universally to one calling—that of carpentry. They work in a very primitive fashion, constructing their own tools, and employing their toes as well as their fingers in the manipulation of them. Although not very skilful in designing, they are clever workmen and carve beautifully. Some of their cabinet work is exquisite ; but the chief industry of the village is the making of cheap furniture. Thousands of tables, chairs, couches and bedsteads, are made in the course of the year, under palm-thatched sheds on the banks of a beautiful lagoon.

ENTERTAINED BY THE CARPENTERS.

These workshops, embowered in the most luxuriant foliage, are so unlike the furniture factories of the western world, the work is carried on so patiently, and the surroundings are so fascinating, that we scarcely realise that the earnest business of life is being carried on. Indeed, there is no earnest diligence, hard work, or hurry and bustle, as in Europe. A shilling a day provides the wherewithal for the workman and his family, and it is permitted to be tardily earned. The methods of the Moratuwa carpenter are consistent with the atmosphere of his enchanting surroundings; for all work in a tropical village is of an *al fresco* nature, and never prosecuted too seriously.

The European visitor is welcomed and shown everything. His presence is always an occasion of great interest and amusement to the non-workers, and especially the children, who flock around him and discuss the curiosity which he displays in their parents' occupations.

Parties of Europeans not infrequently visit Moratuwa to be entertained by the Carpenters, who upon short notice decorate one of their timber boats and place it at the disposal of the party. By this means the many interesting places on the banks of the great lagoon are reached.

The gentleness and courtesy of these people cannot be spoken of too highly, and their appearance quite chimes in with those attributes. Slender frames, small hands and feet, pleasing features and light brown complexions, are their common characteristics. The faces of the young Singhalese women are pleasing, their figures are remarkably good and well-proportioned, and their arms and hands are beautifully formed. An old maid amongst them is almost unknown.* They marry very early, and are often grandmothers at thirty. After that age they soon lose their graceful figures, and although they are generally as long-lived as Europeans, they lose their youthful appearance at an earlier age.

* This statement, which I made in a previous work, was challenged by a reviewer. I am, however, able to repeat it and to add that I have since known many instances. I have now amongst my servants an Ayah who has several grandchildren, while both her mother and grandmother are still alive.

The marriage ceremony amongst the Singhalese is generally celebrated with great festivity, lasting many days, and in some cases even weeks. There is no occasion on which they spend their savings more readily or freely. The widest possible circle of acquaintance is invited to share the round of feasts and entertainments. Moreover, the surest passport to these festive gatherings is similarity of caste rather than of wealth or worldly position.

A pleasant way of making an excursion to Moratuwa is to go by the seaside railway, and drive back in the evening by the Galle Road, through the groves of palms and shrubs which extend the whole distance. The light under these charming avenues after 5 o'clock in the evening is so pleasantly softened by the foliage that the vegetation is then seen to the greatest advantage.

As we pass through the villages, the groups of idle and contented folk seem quite in harmony with the features of the landscape. The naked little urchins frolic everywhere, their well-nourished condition indicating plenty, and their merry voices happy content.

A few miles south of Moratuwa, the beautiful road which we described on page 40, or the railway which runs between it and the sea, brings us to the large village of Panedure. Here is another estuary of great extent and almost unrivalled beauty (see photograph on page 39). So frequent are these calm sheets of water on the coast, from Negombo to Kalutara, that the Dutch took advantage of them to facilitate the construction of canals, which they opened in a continuous line for sixty miles. These works still exist; but however useful they were to

A SINGHALESE WEDDING PARTY.

the Dutch two centuries ago, the British prefer the metalled highways which they have constructed in place of them.

Kalutara, thirty miles south of Colombo, is the next place of importance. Here is the mouth of the Kaluganga or Black River, which is navigable for 40 miles, to Ratnapura, the city of gems. The river traffic is effected with great ease, and is serviceable alike for passengers and produce. The scenery is characteristic of everything in the western lowlands, and the wealth of fine trees—tamarinds, jaks, talipots, kitools, and coconuts—is remarkable.

The town of Kalutara is one of the most salubrious in Ceylon; it faces the sea-breeze from the south-west, and were it not for the fact that Ceylon has an abundance of sanitaria it would doubtless be a favourite resort of Europeans. The Dutch held it in high esteem, not only for its salubrity and the beauty and grandeur of its surrounding scenery, but for its trading facilities. They constructed a considerable fort, which commanded the entrance of the river. This has long been dismantled; but the remains are sufficiently interesting to attract the visitor.

Within the last fifteen years Kalutara has developed great importance as a tea-growing district, and boasts of about seventy flourishing estates under cultivation of this product.

Bentotte, a village between Kalutara and Galle, is notable for honeymoons and oysters. The rest-house is one of the coolest on the coast, and very prettily situated on a point of the beach where the river forms its junction with the sea. The facilities of quiet seclusion, a table supplied with all the

DUTCH GATEWAY AT GALLE.

luxuries of the province, and the pretty scenery of the district frequently attract the European brides and bridegrooms of Ceylon.

Galle, famous in history and noted in commerce for its natural harbour, next claims our attention. For upwards of a thousand years before Colombo assumed any importance as an emporium, Galle was known as such to the eastern world. The places hitherto visited by us have for the most part greatly changed in character during the last fifty years, and the descriptions of them by earlier writers would not hold good to-day. But this venerable port of the south is an exception, and the visitor will find very little at variance with Sir Emerson Tennent's account, published in the middle of the century.

"No traveller fresh from Europe," says Tennent, "will ever part with the impression left by his first gaze upon tropical scenery as it is displayed in the bay and the wooded hills that encircle it; for, although Galle is surpassed both in grandeur and beauty by places afterwards seen in the island, still the feeling of admiration and wonder called forth by its loveliness remains vivid and unimpaired. If, as is frequently the case, the ship approaches the land at daybreak, the view recalls, but in an intensified degree, the emotions excited in childhood by the slow rising of the curtain in a darkened theatre to disclose some magical triumph of the painter's fancy, in all the luxury of colouring and all the glory of light. The sea, blue as sapphire, breaks upon the fortified rocks which form the entrance to the harbour; the headlands are bright with verdure; and the yellow strand is shaded by palm trees that incline towards the sea, and bend their crowns above the water. The shore is gemmed with flowers, the hills behind are draped with forests of perennial green; and far in the distance rises the zone of purple hills, above which towers the sacred mountain of Adam's Peak, with its summit enveloped in clouds.

"But the interest of the place is not confined to the mere loveliness of its scenery. Galle is by far the most venerable emporium of foreign trade now existing in the universe; it was the resort of merchant ships at the earliest dawn of commerce, and it is destined to be the centre to which will hereafter converge all the rays of navigation, intersecting the Indian Ocean, and connecting the races of Europe and Asia." This prophecy, however, is not likely to be fulfilled, since Colombo, with its artificial harbour, has already usurped the position.

Tennent's account of the commercial importance of Galle in early times is of great interest: "Galle was the 'Kalah' at which the Arabians in the reign of Haroun Alraschid met the junks of the Chinese, and brought back gems, silks, and spices from Serendib to Bassora. The Sabæans, centuries before, included Ceylon in the rich trade which they prosecuted with India, and Galle was probably the furthest point eastward ever reached by the Persians, by the Greeks of the Lower Empire, by the Romans, and by the Egyptian mariners of Berenice, under the Ptolemies. But an interest deeper still attaches to this portion of Ceylon, inasmuch as it seems more than probable that *the long-sought locality of Tarshish may be found to be identical with that of Point de Galle.*

"A careful perusal of the Scripture narrative

THE SEA COAST AT GALLE.

suggests the conclusion that there were two places at least to which the Phœnicians traded, each of which bore the name of Tarshish: one to the north-west, whence they brought tin, iron and lead; and another to the east, which supplied them with ivory and gold. Bochart was not the first who rejected the idea of the *latter* being situated at the mouth of Guadalquiver; and intimated that it must be sought for in the direction of India; but he was the first who conjectured that Ophir was Koudramalie, on the north-west of Ceylon, and that the Eastern Tarshish must have been somewhere in the vicinity of Cape Comorin. His general inference was correct and irresistible from the tenor of the sacred writings; but from want of topographical knowledge, Bochart was in error as to the actual localities. Gold is not to be found at Koudramalie; and Comorin, being neither an island nor a place of trade, does not correspond to the requirements of Tarshish. Subsequent investigation has served to establish the claim of Malacca to be the golden land of Solomon, and Tarshish, which lay in the track between the Arabian Gulf and Ophir, is recognisable in the great emporium of Ceylon.

"The ships intended for the voyage were built by Solomon at 'Ezion-geber on the shores of the Red Sea,' the rowers coasted along the shores of Arabia and the Persian Gulf, headed by an east wind.

"Tarshish, the port for which they were bound, would appear to have been situated in an island, governed by kings, and carrying on an extensive foreign trade. The voyage occupied three years in going and returning from the Red Sea, and the cargoes brought home to Ezion-geber consisted of gold and silver, ivory, apes, and peacocks. *Gold* could have been shipped at Galle from the vessels which brought it from Ophir, *silver* spread into plates," which is particularised by Jeremiah as an export of Tarshish, is one of the substances on which the sacred books of the Singhalese are even now inscribed; *ivory* is found in Ceylon, and must have been both abundant and full grown there before the discovery of gunpowder led to the wanton destruction of elephants; *apes* are indigenous to the island, and *peafowl* are found there in numbers. It is very remarkable, too, that the terms by which these articles are designated in the Hebrew Scriptures, are identical with the Tamil names, by which some of them are called in Ceylon to the present day: thus *tukeyim*, which is rendered "peacocks" in one version, may be recognised in *tokei*, the modern name for these birds; "*kapi*" apes is the same in both languages, and the Sanskrit "*ibha*" ivory, is identical with the Tamil "*ibam*."

"Thus by geographical position, by indigenous productions, and by the fact of its having been from time immemorial the resort of merchant ships from Egypt, Arabia, and Persia on the one side, and India, Java, and China on the other, Galle seems to present a combination of every particular essential to determine the problem so long undecided in biblical dialectics, and thus to present data for inferring its identity with the Tarshish of the sacred historians, the great eastern mart so long frequented by the ships of Tyre and Judea."

In modern times Galle has been the mart of Portugal and afterwards of Holland. The extensive fort constructed by the Dutch is still one of the chief

A BIT OF OLD DUTCH GALLE.

features of the place and encloses the modern town. Although dismantled, few portions of it have been destroyed, and the remains add greatly to the picturesque character of the landscape. Amongst a large number of interesting remains of the Dutch period are the gateway of the fortress, the present entrance from the harbour, and the Dutch church, both of which we illustrate. A steep and shady

OLD GATE STREET, GALLE.

street known as Old Gate Street ascends to the principal part of the town.

The most flourishing period of Galle during the British occupation was that immediately preceding the construction of the harbour at Colombo. Then Galle obtained a large share of the modern steamship trade. Its harbour was always considered dangerous, owing to the rocks and currents about the mouth; but it was preferred to the open roadstead of Colombo, and the P. & O. and other important Companies made use of it. Passengers for Colombo were landed at Galle, and a coach service provided them with the means of reaching their destination.

The town was alive with such trade as passengers

MIDDLE STREET, GALLE.

bring, besides the trade of shipping merchants. The local manufacturers of jewellery and tortoise-shell ornaments, for which Galle has always been famous, met the strangers on arrival and did a thriving business. In fact, Galle was a miniature of what Colombo is to-day. But the new harbour of Colombo sealed its fate. The manufacturers now send their wares to Colombo, and the merchants have to a great extent migrated thither. The local prosperity of Galle has therefore had a serious check; its fine hotel knows no "passenger days," its bazaars are quiet and its streets have lost their whilom busy aspect. Nevertheless, it is the seat of administration of a large, populous and thriving province, and must always remain a place of considerable importance. Its share of commerce will probably increase as

LIGHTHOUSE STREET, GALLE.

cultivation and mining still further extend. It is a great centre of the coconut industry which has in recent years developed to a remarkable degree and is likely still further to increase.

The visitor will be impressed with the cleanliness no less than the picturesque character of the streets, which are shaded by Suriya trees. The buildings, as will be seen from our photographs, are substantial and well-kept, some of the houses of the wealthier residents being admirably planned for coolness. Lighthouse Street contains the humbler dwellings; but even here the houses are spacious and each has along the entire front a deep verandah supported on pillars to create shade. This street probably presented the same appearance during the presence of the Dutch. The English Church of All Saints', visible in our photograph of Church Street, is the

THE ENGLISH CHURCH, GALLE.

finest in Ceylon, both in its architectural features and the quality of its construction.

The old Dutch Church, paved with tombstones and hung with mural monuments of the seventeenth and eighteenth centuries, has now an antiquarian interest. It is still used by the Presbyterian section of the inhabitants, and is well worth the attention of the visitor as a very good specimen of the places of worship which the Dutch erected wherever they formed a settlement. Churches and forts are the abiding evidences of the solid determination of the Dutch to remain in Ceylon.

They had come to stay, and consequently spared no cost or trouble to make their buildings of a permanent character. The British colonists, on the other hand, make Ceylon their temporary home, and seldom intend to die there; consequently they do not display great enthusiasm for permanent institutions;

THE DUTCH CHURCH, GALLE.

indeed, a whole century has passed without any attempt to build a cathedral worthy of the name, and with the exception of Galle there is scarcely a beautiful English church in the country.

The most curious relic of the Dutch which still exists at Galle is, strange to say, a living creature. The grand old tortoise whose portrait we reproduce is supposed to have belonged to one of the Dutch Governors some two hundred years ago. What the exact age of this venerable specimen of animal longevity is I cannot say, but it is probably a couple of centuries. He is at present in the possession of Mr. J. Reddie-Black, and has the run of the

A LIVING RELIC OF THE DUTCH.

splendid grounds of his country house at Hirimbura, near Galle. He is very docile and ever ready to attract the attention of anyone who is likely to offer him a plantain. His enormous size may be gathered from comparison with the fifteen-year-old boy who stands near him. He would find no difficulty in carrying several such boys upon his back at one time.

We have said that Galle is a centre of the coconut industry, and we have seen how the whole neighbourhood is covered with palms which shade every road and even droop right over the sea. Nowhere are we impressed so much by the scenery of this palm-

"THE SAND IS CARPETED WITH VERDURE."

land as here; the coast, as will be seen in our photographs, is densely bordered by the tall ring-marked stems of the coconut, with their magnificent crowns of fronds and fruit; and beneath them even the sand is carpeted with verdure right down to the water's edge. This feature of the southern shores always strikes the stranger as being singularly beautiful, although the appreciation of the resident is perhaps dulled by the frequent vision of all that is most beautiful in tropical landscapes. There is no place in the world in which the coconut palm flourishes as it does in Ceylon, and there is no part of Ceylon where it flourishes better than upon the southern coast. The visitor, in travelling from Galle to Matara, will have his attention constantly arrested by some strange process of manufacture being carried on in connection with the coconut. Its uses are so many that we cannot even enumerate them here; but a few statistics from Mr. John Ferguson's wonderful "Handbook" will give some idea of the increasing importance of the industry. "The maximum value of products of the coconut palm annually exported may be taken at about the following figures:—Oil, £500,000; Coir, £80,000; Arrack, £25,000; Copra (the dried kernel sent to India for native food and latterly to France to be expressed), £180,000; Nuts, £25,000; Poonac, £50,000; desiccated Coconut and miscellaneous products, £120,000 =say £1,000,000—while the value of the produce locally consumed must be taken from eight to ten million rupees per annum, and the market value of the area covered with coconuts approximates probably to twelve millions sterling. The extended local use, as well as cultivation, of coconuts is certain to go on with Railway Extension and the development of the coast districts as well as of part of the interior of the island—Ceylon Coconut Oil in London has varied from average £38 per ton in 1877 to £28 in 1893; Copperah has run from £15 to £18 in same time."

Tradition ascribes the discovery of the coconut tree in Ceylon to a vision of Kushta Rajah, a leper king, who was advised that if he visited a venerated Buddhist shrine at Weligama he would be cured of his affliction. Weligama is the next stage of our journey along the south coast; and here we may see a gigantic statue of Kushta carved in a huge boulder of granite. The legend as related by the chief priest at Weligama is as follows:—A Singhalese king became afflicted with a loathsome cutaneous disease which almost deprived him of human appearance. His people resorted to sacrifices in the hope of appeasing the angry demon who

"THEIR TOPS APPEARED CROWNED WITH TUFTS OF FEATHERY LEAVES."

was supposed to be the author of the king's sufferings. But the Rajah objected to the diabolical ceremonies on his behalf, and with due humility made offerings at the shrine of Buddha. He then fell into a trance, during which a vision represented to him a large expanse of water bordered by trees of a rare kind, such as he had never before seen; for instead of branches spreading from the trunks in various directions their tops appeared crowned with tufts of feathery leaves. (The coconut is supposed to have been unknown in Ceylon at this period.) The nature of this vision deeply impressed the Rajah and caused him to renew his Buddhist devotions. Next, a cobra, the sacred snake of Buddhism, appeared to him and thrice lapped water from his drinking vessel. He then slept again, and his vision recurred, with the additional appearance of the father of Buddha, who thus accosted him: "From ignorance of the sacredness of the ground over which the God's favorite tree casts its honored shade, thou once didst omit the usual respect due to it from all his creatures. Its deeply pointed leaf distinguishes it above all other trees as sacred to Buddha; and, under another tree of the same heavenly character, thou now liest a leprous mass, which disease at the great Deity's command, the impurity of the red water within the large and small rivers of thy body has brought upon thee. But since the sacred and kind snake, the shelterer of the God Buddha when on earth, has thrice partaken of thy drink, thou wilt derive health and long life by obeying the high commands which I now bear thee. In that direction [pointing to the southward] lies thy remedy. One hundred hours' journey will bring thee to those trees, which thou shalt see in reality, and taste their fruits to thy benefit; but as on the top only they are produced, by fire only can they be obtained. The inside, of transparent liquid, and of innocent pulp, must be thy sole diet, till thrice the Great Moon (*Maha Handah*) shall have given and refused her light:—at the expiration of that time, disease will leave thee, and thou wilt be clean again."

The one hundred hours' journey having been

THE NIL-GANGA AT MATARA.

miraculously performed, for it had been accomplished without fatigue either to himself or attendants, the long and anxiously anticipated view of that boundless expanse of blue water, and on its margin immense groves of trees, with crests of leaves (which he then for the first time perceived to be large fronds), gratified his astonished and delighted sight, as his visions had foretold. Beneath the fronds, sheltered from the vertical sun, hung large clusters of fruit, much larger than any he had ever seen in his own country of the interior, of which, the colour of some was green, yellow, and orange, and of others, approaching to black.

The novel fruit was opened and partaken of. The liquid within the nuts was sweet and delicious, while the fleshy part was found to be cool and grateful food. The leprosy left the Rajah, and in commemoration of the event he carved the gigantic figure of himself which is now regarded as one of the most curious relics of antiquity in Ceylon.*

Matara is a beautiful and interesting town of some twenty thousand inhabitants lying at the mouth of the Nil-ganga or Blue River, which flows into the sea within four miles of Dondra Head, the southernmost point of the island. Apart from the beauty of the river, which like all others in Ceylon is bordered on either bank with the richest vegetation, the points of interest in Matara are Dutch Antiquarian; and as we are leaving antiquities almost unnoticed in this volume a slight reference to them must suffice.

* From the account of Mr. J. W. Bennett, of the Ceylon Civil Service, published in 1843.

There are two forts and an old Dutch Church still in good preservation to testify to the importance with which Matara was regarded in the seventeenth and eighteenth centuries. The smaller of the forts is of the well-known star formation. It was built by Governor Van Eck in 1763. The gateway is in particularly good preservation, and although the arms above the door are carved in wood every detail is still perfect. At the present time this star fort serves as the residence of the officer of the Public Works for the Matara district.

The larger fort consists of extensive stone and coral works facing the sea and extending inwards on the south till they meet the river, which forms part of the defences. Within the enclosure are most of the official buildings of the place, including the Courts, the Kachcheri, and the residence of the Assistant Government Agent. To these buildings must be added the Rest-house which is important to travellers and will be found very comfortable. The appearance of the fort, from within, is distinctly park-like and picturesque owing to the beautiful trees which have been introduced in recent years. These afford delightful shade and render a stroll beneath them pleasant when the sun would not permit of walking in the open.

The land around Matara is extremely fertile and no place could be more abundantly supplied with food, especially fish, the variety of which is very large. The neighbourhood affords most delightful walks and drives through the finest avenues of umbrageous trees to be met with in Ceylon. Nothing surprises the visitor more than this feature of complete shade upon the roads of the extreme

BATHING ON THE BANKS OF THE NIL-GANGA

south of the island, and in no part is it more grateful than upon the road from Matara to Tangalla, whither we shall presently proceed.

Our picture of the bathing-place on the banks of the Nil-ganga possesses one feature which may seem curious to the European who is not acquainted with tropical rivers—the fence of large stakes constructed to keep out the crocodiles. Without this, bathing would be unsafe and would probably be indulged in at the cost of many a human life and great feasting on the part of the "crocs." This photograph also presents a typical scene in the background from which some idea may be gathered of the recreation grounds of a southern town in Ceylon. Here golf and cricket claim their votaries as in larger places, and facilities for enjoying these games are not wanting.

We have already exceeded the dimensions originally planned for this book, and although the places of interest are by no means exhausted we must be content to end our peregrinations at Tangalla, an exceedingly attractive village about twenty miles beyond Matara. The drive thither is full of interest. No sooner do we get out of the town than the perfume of citronella calls our attention to an industry which we have not before seen.

Citronella grows without much care or attention on the poorest land, and since there is a large demand for the essential oil of this grass, for use in perfumery, it has answered the purpose of the agriculturists between Matara and Tangalla to spread its cultivation over about twenty thousand acres of land which would otherwise have remained fallow. For many years a high price was obtained for the oil, but latterly it has fallen so low as to render the cultivation of citronella almost unprofitable. The wily cultivator sought to meet his misfortune by adulteration; but this only brought the Ceylon product into disrepute. Judging, however, from the number of distilleries which we see by the roadside, we do not doubt but that there is still some remuneration for the grower of citronella.

At the fourth mile of our coach journey we arrive at the southern extremity of Ceylon—Dondra Head A visit to the lighthouse is well repaid by the beautiful scenery of the coast; but the chief attraction is to be found in the very ancient ruins which are spread over a considerable area. Dondra has been held sacred by both Hindoos and Buddhists from very early times. In the Portuguese period (16th century) it was the most renowned place of pilgrimage in Ceylon. From the sea the temple had the appearance of a city. The pagoda was richly decorated and roofed with gilded copper. Its magnificence, however, only excited the rapacity of the ruthless Portuguese, who tore down its thousands of statues and demolished its colonnades. A finely carved stone doorway and a large number of handsome columns of granite are all that now remain.

There is still an annual pilgrimage made to this sacred place; but it is now commonly known as Dondra fair, and partakes of the nature of a holiday. A large camp is formed by the erection of temporary sheds roofed with leaves of the talipot palm; and here thousands of natives assemble, making day and night hideous by the blowing of chank shells and the beating of tom-toms. The visitor who arrives at the time of this fair will be amused at the sight

THE SOUTH COAST, NEAR TANGALLA.

of such picturesque crowds and the weird ceremonies which they perform, but will probably be glad to get away from the torturous music.

The drive to Tangalla is chiefly interesting for the lovely seascapes which burst upon the gaze at frequent intervals. Our photograph fairly represents the general character of this part of the south coast. The coves and bays are separated by precipitous headlands, which are always well covered with vegetation and crowned with beautiful palms.

Tangalla itself exhibits one of the finest bays in Ceylon, being four miles in extent between the headlands. It has the appearance of a magnificent harbour, being so well protected that the water is always calm and no surf breaks upon the shore, but it is, in fact, a very dangerous bay for shipping, owing to its numerous coral reefs and sand banks.

The ubiquitous Dutch fort commands the best views of Tangalla, but is itself a blot upon the landscape, and its present use, as a district prison, harmonizes with its ugly appearance. The village, on the other hand, is exceedingly pretty, and will not fail to charm the visitor.

It remains now only to say that should the reader who has accompanied me through these pages be induced to put my descriptions to the test of personal experience, I do not fear the result; while my object in presenting this volume to the public will be thereby realised.

INDEX.

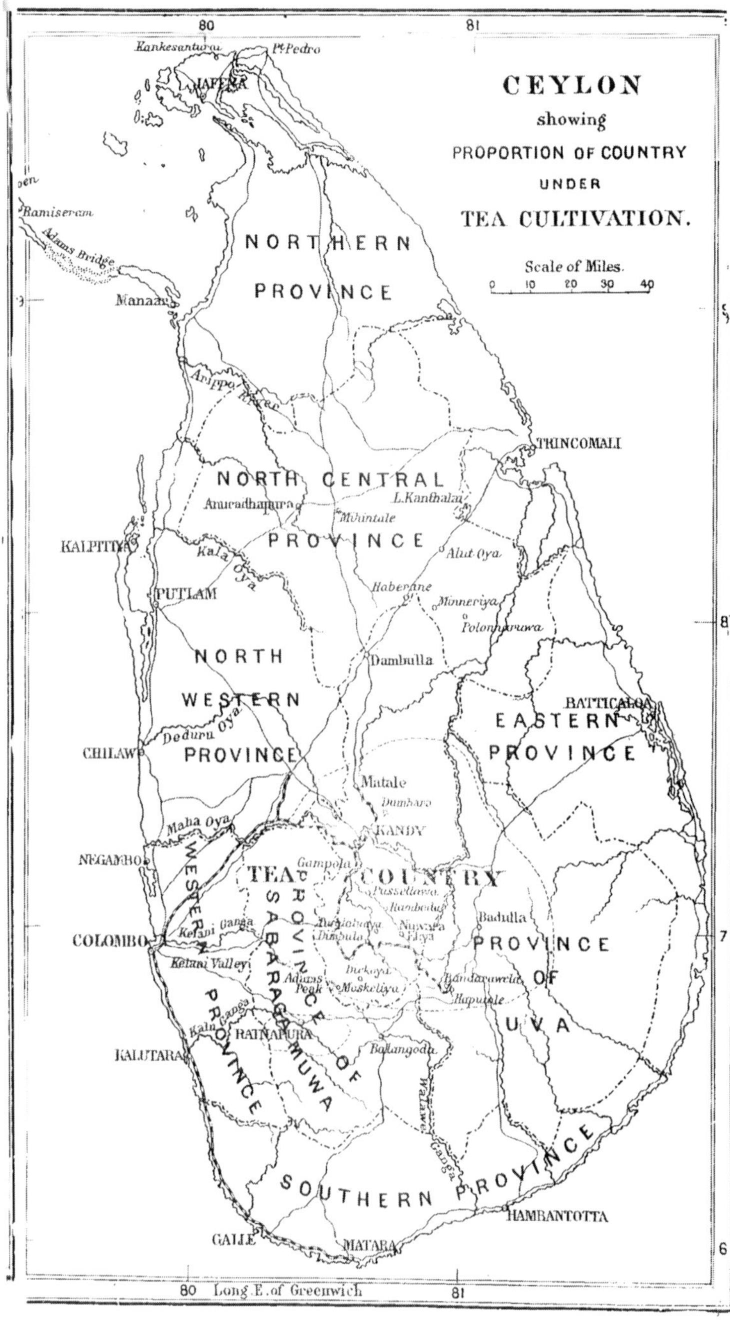

CEYLON
showing
PROPORTION OF COUNTRY
UNDER
TEA CULTIVATION.
Scale of Miles.
0 10 20 30 40
80
81
Kankesanturai
Pt. Pedro
JAFFNA
Ramiseram
Adams Bridge
Manaar
NORTHERN PROVINCE
Arippo River
TRINCOMALI
NORTH CENTRAL PROVINCE
Anuradhapura
Mihintale
L. Kanthalai
Alut Oya
KALPITIYA
Kala Oya
PUTLAM
Haberane
Minneriya
Polonnaruwa
NORTH WESTERN PROVINCE
Dambulla
BATTICALOA
EASTERN PROVINCE
Deduru Oya
CHILAW
Matale
Dumbara
KANDY
Maha Oya
NEGAMBO
TEA COUNTRY
Gampola
Pussellawa
Rambodde
Badulla
Kelani Ganga
COLOMBO
Dimbula
Nuwara Eliya
PROVINCE OF UVA
WESTERN PROVINCE
Kelani Valley
PROVINCE OF SABARAGAMUWA
Adams Peak
Dickoya
Maskeliya
Bandarawela
Haputale
Kalu Ganga
RATNAPURA
KALUTARA
Balangoda
Walawe Ganga
SOUTHERN PROVINCE
HAMBANTOTTA
GALLE
MATARA
8
7
6
Long. E. of Greenwich